D0532302

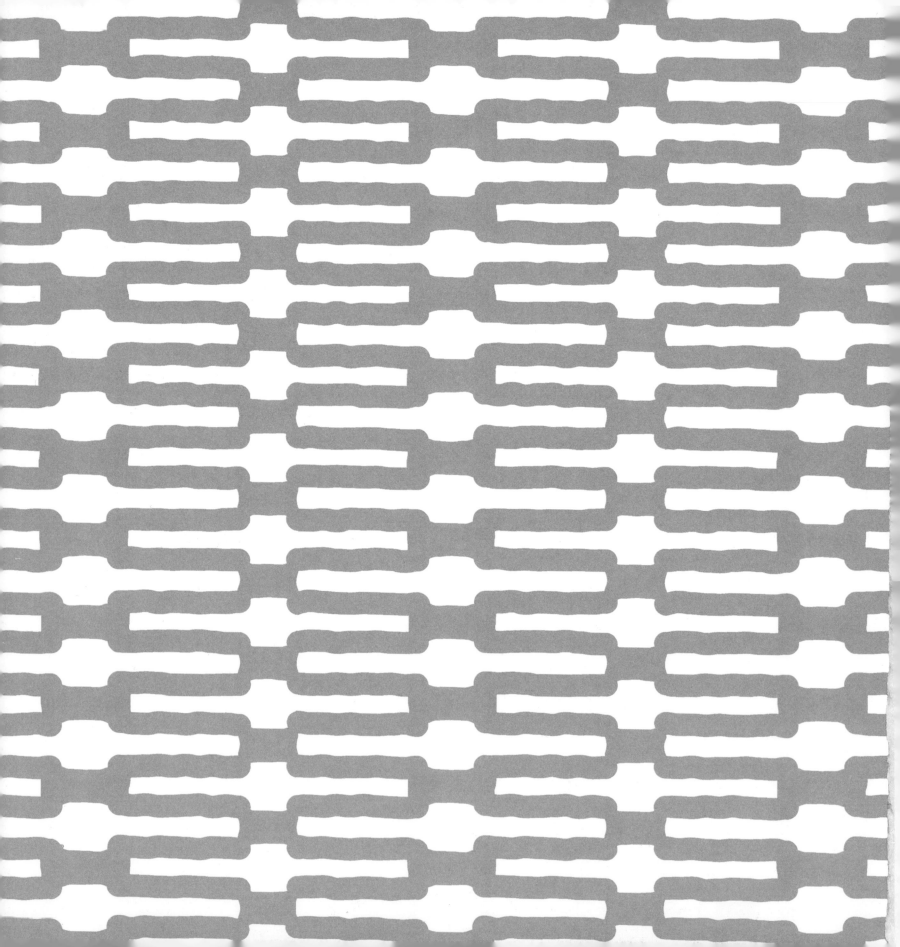

fresh american spaces

ROMANTIC · NUANCED · HAPPY · CULTURED · EXUBERANT

annie selke

Clarkson Potter/Publishers
New York

Principal room photography and room detail photography
by **Kindra Clineff**
Photographs on pages 58 (bottom right), 59 (top left), 60, 63, 90–91 by
Andrew Bordwin; photographs on pages 11, 12 (bottom right), 190
(top center and middle right), 191 (center right), 192, 195, 204–5, 238
by **Laura Moss**
All other photographs provided by **The Annie Selke Companies**

Published in the United States by Clarkson Potter/Publishers,
an imprint of the Crown Publishing Group, a division of
Random House, Inc., New York.
www.crownpublishing.com
www.clarksonpotter.com

CLARKSON POTTER is a trademark and POTTER
with colophon is a registered trademark of Random House, Inc.

Library of Congress Cataloging-in-Publication Data
Selke, Annie.
    Fresh American spaces: romantic, nuanced, happy, cultured,
exuberant/Annie Selke. —1st ed.
        p.   cm.
    1. Interior decoration—United States—History—21st century.
I. Title.
NK2004.15.S45   2011
747—dc22   2010052623

ISBN 978-0-307-71606-4

Printed in China

10 9 8 7 6 5 4 3 2 1

First Edition

fresh american spaces

For Mum and Charlotte,
with big love

And to the doggelers—
Dash, Daisy, and
Emmet—
for keeping me
grounded, giggling,
and a bit grubby

contents

happy preppy

nuanced neutral

cultured eclectic

introduction

think we all deserve a home that makes us happy. For me that doesn't mean fancy or over the top; it means filling your life with people, pets, and things you love, and creating a haven of comfort that strikes the balance between fashion and functionality.

Design is my life. It is my passion and my profession, and for me this book represents a cheerful intersection of the two. I have always been an eyes-wide-open, soak-it-all-up-like-a-sponge kind of gal, and now it's time to squeeze that sponge onto the pages that follow!

Inside you will find five distinct design/lifestyle perspectives, all of which I consider Fresh American. Each has its origins in the gazillion ideas that live happily in my head and in the products I design for my home furnishing companies: Pine Cone Hill, Dash and Albert Rug Company, and Annie Selke Home. In defining these five styles, I have drawn on a lifetime of visual imagery—as I said, I'm a sponge—and on thoughts I've had on decorating and life lessons I've learned along the way.

I look to the past for the endless inspiration it offers, plucking the pretty and the practical. I analyze the present for trends in lifestyle, significant shifts in consciousness, and clues for how people live now. I keep an eye on fashion's emerging colors and fabrics, and then I assess and decide how to mix, blend, and answer future lifestyle needs. What will be a fad and what will continue long after we're gone?

Fresh American is a thoroughly modern point of view. Moving beyond traditional notions of good taste, this aesthetic encourages a more democratic and accessible approach to home decorating, in which the golden rules of design and our real-life comfort and joy are taken into account in equal measure.

"Fresh" is the willingness to embrace new ideas, styles, and colors. "American" means freedom of choice and freedom of expression. There is no one correct style; you can find your own approach, making personal choices that reflect who you are and how you want to live and putting them together in a unique, forward-looking environment that meets your needs—practically and aesthetically.

You will be introduced to:

EVERYDAY EXUBERANCE. Color, color, and more color! Awaken your inner child by using it confidently and creatively.

REFINED ROMANTIC. Romance isn't dead! It's alive and well; just updated and refined to sleek, not sickly-sweet.

HAPPY PREPPY. Tradition with a twist! A chipper world where form follows function and practicality takes center stage, enlivened by a perky, primary palette.

NUANCED NEUTRAL. Anything but colorless! Create a beautiful, never-bland environment by exploring the range of colors from black to white, brown to ivory, and all the myriad shades in between, and enhance interest by layering colors, fabrics, textures, and shapes.

CULTURED ECLECTIC. Wear your passions on your sleeve! Curate your personal peculiarities into a space that is a rich and true reflection of what you love.

Use this book as a diagnostic tool: Find the specific styles that resonate with you and then take an à la carte approach. Are you Cultured Eclectic with a dash of Refined Romantic, or are you a committed Happy Prepster? Does Nuanced Neutral layered with Everyday Exuberance rock your world? The point is to explore what works for you—mix and match, borrow and blend—until you discover your own Fresh American style.

Enjoy the possibilities.

everyday
exuberance

don't hide your bright under a bushel

One of the great mysteries I've yet to solve is why so many people fear having too much color in their homes. We certainly never tire of vibrant color in every other aspect of our lives. There's no such thing as overdosing on blue skies, pink sunsets, red berries, green mountains, or golden sunshine.

Vibrant color evokes and engenders optimism. It's energizing and uplifting. Color seems to strike a chord with the youthful side of our personalities, fostering a childlike sense of wonder.

Adults need the stimulation and excitement of a colorful environment as much as or more than children do. You may have to study spreadsheets during the day instead of getting to finger-paint and play with clay, but after work don't you want to set your spirit free?

Happiness is priceless, and paint is cheap. Why not put my theory to the test and paint a single wall of one room your favorite color? The risk-to-reward ratio is huge. There is no area too big or too small to benefit from an infusion of color. There is no style of house that is immune to its power. Think of the colonial houses in historic Williamsburg, with their color-saturated walls, or the bold, graphic murals of Sol LeWitt that were designed to complement modernist architecture.

Unlike the other chapters, in which we combine four distinct elements, the overarching element of Everyday Exuberant interiors is color, color, and, yes, more color. In this chapter you will see a range of ways in which to introduce it, from ephemeral touches, to semi-permanent additions, to whole-hog commitment. You will experience a range of exuberant rooms, all of them everyday spaces that have been transformed with varying degrees of color. They are sassy and sophisticated; nothing crazy, just colorful. You'll see a neutral room layered with pops of color. You'll view an example of white used as a backdrop for a two-tone palette. And you'll be able to consider how you feel about full-on saturation. Seeing these interiors will allow you to move along the color path, gauging your tolerance as you go, and then help you make a plan for your own home.

As you begin to experiment, remember that you don't need to be madcap to be bold. Start by adding exuberant colors in small, judicious doses—colorful accents such as a zippy pair of pillows, a multicolor striped rug, a single jewel-tone throw over a brown leather chair. I bet you'll find these initial strokes of color invigorating. You can keep adding and layering on more color (as you do with a summer bouquet of dahlias, zinnias, and snapdragons) until you find your desired exuberance level. I guarantee that adding more exhilarating colors to your home will brighten the gloomiest of days!

everyday exuberance
fabrics

Exuberant fabrics provide a wonderful jumping-off point for any decorating scheme, as they already contain a cohesive palette that shows similarly saturated colors.

MULTI PRINTS. I recommend choosing an exuberant multicolored print to establish a palette, a sensibility, and an organizing principle for your scheme. Remember, too much of a good thing dilutes its impact. Instead, the print might appear only on a statement chair and a pair of pillows. Once you've chosen the "big idea" fabric, look for "friends" that work happily with the colors and the overall feel of the multi print.

SMALLER-SCALE MULTI PRINTS. A smaller-scale coordinated print is a nice way to introduce the multicolored palette into the room in a more subtle way. Be sure to incorporate other fabrics (such as a solid or a simple two-tone print) into the scheme if you are using two intentionally coordinated patterns, so the overall effect isn't too matchy-matchy.

STRIPES. Use stripes to provide a linear counterpart for a bold print. Smaller-scale stripes are preferable for smaller pieces, as it becomes hard on the eyes to take in too large an expanse of small stripes. Use larger-scale stripes on larger pieces such as sofas or for curtains.

TWO-TONE PRINTS AND WOVENS. These are a designer's best friend. They work just about anywhere you would consider using a solid, but they add more interest. Often available in medium to small scales, they make great throw pillows or upholstery for pieces that are multiples, such as dining chairs, and can also work well for window treatments.

SOLIDS. Look for distinguished fabrics in solid colors plucked from your multi print. Choose options that have some texture and/or are inviting to the touch, such as brushed twill, linen, velvet, ultra-suede, real suede, leather, and mohair.

color

Making a commitment to color can be daunting. Relax. Start small. Go crazy with a splashy bouquet of flowers. Try out various combinations of colors, noting which you like best. If the flowers lift your spirit, then you're ready to move on to other easy-to-introduce-and-swap textile accessories, such as pillows, bath and kitchen towels, napkins, tablecloths, and bed linens. Elevate and energize other-wise routine basics by adding colorful touches of happy trim.

ART AND OBJECTS. Brilliantly colored artwork, posters, and objects like these snappy Chinese butterfly kites will quickly brighten any blank wall. Consider hanging other colorful collections you have.

TEXTILE ACCESSORIES. Decorative pillows and throws add zest and joie de vivre to a room. Everything from a chair to a bed, a banquette to a sofa, is happier with brightly colored friends to call its own. There are so many fabulous options to choose from. Have fun and find things you love. I often look to hand-hewn ethnic or vividly colored vintage textiles to sew into pillows or drape over a sofa. They make a more personal and usually less expensive alternative, and add a dash of dazzle to neutral upholstery.

TABLEWARE. Dishes, vases, pitchers, candles, and other everyday objects are readily available in a rainbow of colors. Plastic, pottery, paper, you name it—setting a tantalizing table is a wonderful way to start experimenting with color.

color

If you have successfully introduced colorful accessories into your world, you are now ready for some bigger, more permanent, possibly pricier expressions, such as furniture, upholstery, window treatments, and lamps.

FURNITURE IN BOLD SOLIDS. Sassy solids add instant panache on painted wood or upholstered furniture. Choose your pop of color carefully, using it on a piece with a shape noteworthy enough to be highlighted. Brightly hued ultrasuede, leather, and canvas make good choices for upholstery.

UPHOLSTERY IN EXUBERANT PATTERNS. When you add vivid patterned furniture, it is generally best to let it be the statement piece and to choose other fabrics, rugs, or objects in the room to play off of it. It is possible to create effective spaces by heaping pattern on pattern, but if patterns are not handled thoughtfully, the result can easily look aimless and messy.

WINDOW TREATMENTS. Curtains are a natural place to introduce colorful pattern. Reserve some extra fabric to use somewhere else in the space, to make your choice seem more intentional. For an unexpected wow, try a fabulous, sleekly modern shade such as this one (opposite) from Surface View (see resources).

LAMPS. Lamps come in all shapes, sizes, and yes, colors! Choose one in a highlight shade that is not the dominant color in the room, so it pops. Don't forget that lampshades offer a great opportunity for introducing some wonderfully wacky or colorful trim.

color

If you've moved from small accessories to bold color statements and are now ready to make a real commitment to color, take the plunge. A little preparation will ensure that you won't regret it.

WALLS. Paint is the quickest, least expensive way to add color to your walls. It can also be changed without too much difficulty. Before deciding on a hue, try a quart or the new mini color samples on the market, and paint each color on large pieces of foam core. Then look at them in the space at various times of day and decide which color you like best. A word about coordination: Any color you can conjure can usually be mixed to match, so bring your chosen fabrics or other inspiration with you when you go to choose paint.

I love wallpaper, and it can make a room sing, but I recommend you hang a large sample on your wall for a few weeks before committing to a colorful pattern. Use a guest room or bathroom as your lab.

TILE. Tile can be very effective in a bath or kitchen. It is available in a yummy selection of solid and multicolored hues. Live with a sample before you buy, and test it in the sink to see how water spots show up on it. The darker the color, the more you will be wiping down those pesky spots. I speak from experience here.

FLOORS. Color is wonderful underfoot. Try painting a distressed or uninteresting wood floor in a fun solid or a two-tone diamond or checkerboard pattern.

AREA RUGS. Multihued rugs add a welcome shot of pizzazz to any space. The one at right is particularly great because it offers a multitude of colors to work with when coordinating your room.

CARPET. Carpet is available in most any color you can imagine. I have used lavender, coral, and pink carpets in bedrooms, to great effect—the color envelops you in a cozy, friendly way. Patterned carpets are not only fun but also great at hiding dirt!

paint details

Standing in front of a wall of paint chips sends shivers down my spine. I love searching for just the right color for the right job. In your own search, use your imagination, and try various colors on for size. Before you commit to a whole room, start small with a sturdy wood chair, table, or other serviceable item in need of some love. Your local secondhand store, the Goodwill, and your attic are all great sources. Now choose your favorite daring color, paint the object, and behold what an incredible transformation you can make simply by adding a zippy color.

Once you're accustomed to small splashes of color, it's time to take on your walls. Try using happy colors in unexpected places. I painted my front door a fabulous pink from Benjamin Moore called Drop Dead Gorgeous and it makes me happy every day. Perk up traditionally pedestrian, service-oriented spaces; paint the inside of a hall closet a happy shade. I promise you will smile every time you reach for your coat. And who says a garage needs to be a dingy gray? Why not paint yours yellow or orange and park your car in a sunny spot every day of the year? Search out what tickles your fancy, pick up that brush, and have some fun!

1. Pratt & Lambert Midnight Sun

2. Benjamin Moore Spring Moss

3. Benjamin Moore Deep Carnation

4. Benjamin Moore Drop Dead Gorgeous

5. Benjamin Moore Peony

6. Pratt & Lambert Anchusa

7. Benjamin Moore Tequila Lime

8. Pratt & Lambert Paramour

9. Sherwin-Williams Gentian

10. Benjamin Moore Douglas Fir

11. Pratt & Lambert Dutchess Choice

12. Sherwin-Williams Kid's Stuff

13. Benjamin Moore Tomato Red

art smart

In my main living spaces, shown at left and on the following pages, I wanted the vibrancy and energy of artwork to take center stage. For me, dreaming up palettes is easy—in fact, too easy. I can create schemes in my head all day, every day. My problem is settling on just one.

Instead of ignoring this inability to commit, I decided to embrace it by creating an environment that would support a palette that could evolve with my mood and the seasons, and work well with the inevitable shedding of my three white dogs. To start, I honored the house's mid-century roots by sticking to clean-lined furniture, buying a few iconic pieces to help set the modernist stage. I left the soaring windows bare except for subtle, light-controlling shades, and painted the whole room Benjamin Moore Atrium White.

The layout is loft-like, and because the living room and the more casual TV-centric "study" are separated by only a three-sided fireplace, I felt I needed to create a commonality of color and texture to link the spaces and then add differentiations between the two. Taupe linen, conveniently friendly to many a color, used on the sofa and sectional, brindle cowhide on the curvy arm chairs, and deep chocolate leather on the low bench act as the simple solid-colored dress

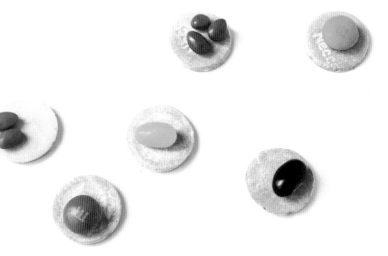

art smart (continued)

waiting to be transformed by carefully chosen accessories. I tossed in some natural-edged wood tables to introduce an organic, slightly unruly element to an otherwise clean-lined concept.

After having exercised all manner of restraint so that the space had the texture and nuance of a great neutral room, it was time to layer on the color. And I knew exactly where to start: with art. Each space is dominated by its canvas. The six-foot-tall abstract in the living room and the naïve painting of the bouquet in the study, while dramatically different, are all about color, and each makes me deeply happy. Both are framed to appear as if floating, in order to let their colors interact freely with the space.

Finding a color common to each painting helped me choose the green rugs used in both spaces. I modeled my choice of accessories, flowers, and plants after the interaction of colors within each painting. Artwork can often inspire multiple potential color schemes, and with small additions and alterations, these rooms take on a fluid and ever-changing element—like the seasons on display outside.

tangerine dream

Like a delicious glass of fresh-squeezed OJ, the bright and happy dining room that follows turns every frown upside down. Drawing the palette from the glorious still life at the center of the room made choosing paint colors a pleasure. The lively orange of the wall, the cheerful pink of the bench, and the bright blue of the chairs were all plucked straight out of the painting.

Every piece of furniture in this room is from a secondhand store—the total bill amounted to less than $400. The unmatched chairs are unified by vivid blue paint, transforming their differences into an interesting design element rather than a flaw. There are a jumble of styles at play—colonial-style chairs and bench, plus a mid-century modern sideboard, and a Scandinavian-inspired trestle table. In their original wood finishes the pieces were a decorating disaster, but painting each one of them erased their history, allowing only their form and color to stand out. Welcome expanses of white give the eye a place to rest, keeping the vivid palette from becoming overwhelming.

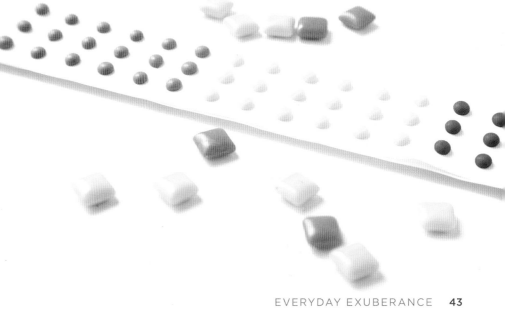

girl whirl

Animated, energetic, and as fresh as the oversize tulips on the personality-packed chair—every inch of the next room exudes optimism. There is no question the space is unabashedly girly, but it isn't juvenile in any way. Its sophistication comes from the interplay of pattern, shapes, and varying shades of the same two colors—in this case, pink and green. This effect can be achieved through any combination of two colors used thoughtfully to avoid a cloying or overly simplistic room. In fact, working within the confines of the two-tone palette forces you to be creative and strike a balance between the colors.

The gallery-like white setting works perfectly to frame the variety of shapes, and it highlights the correlation between the pieces. Though green and pink make an appearance in the rug, blue adds a welcome, dissonant touch that keeps the whole scheme from being too matchy-matchy.

bohemian rhapsody

If you were simply to list the colors used in the following space—lilac, burnt orange, fuchsia, rust, and ochre—I would have to say, "Hmm, I can't quite picture how they would all work together." When I spied this delightfully exotic rug, however, I fell madly, deeply in love with everything about it, and then the palette made all the sense in the world. The combination of colors was stunning, but in an understated way. The fact that all the colors in the rug are of roughly the same intensity keeps any one of them from being overwhelming or jumpy, and as they are woven side by side, none of them dominates. The colors that could become too sweet, the lilac and the pink, are offset by more neutral, rougher earth tones, resulting in a balanced sophistication.

Building from the rug, I chose very traditional English-style upholstery shapes but covered them in vivid fuchsia and rich burnt orange. Then I married them to the rug and to one another by adding the rust and fuchsia Kashmiri crewel embroidery on the pillows (just the right note of Far Eastern flair, which is underscored by the Moroccan table and the window treatments made from Indian dhurries). The gilded table and mirror along with the brass lamps add brightness and act as counterpoints to the dark-framed mirrors and dark chest, finishing off this eclectically exuberant room.

HOW-TO: painting stripes on a wall

1. Select the lightest color of your palette (your base color) and apply it to the entire wall. Outline the stripes on the wall as you want them using a pencil and a level. Stripes of varying width add interest. Using one continuous length of tape per stripe, apply painter's tape along the pencil markings to create even lines. Press the tape firmly to the wall.

2. Paint a second coat of your base color on each stripe and let it dry. This will help fill in accidental gaps. Paint your desired stripe color between the lines, painting over the edge of the tape to ensure total coverage. Allow it to dry before proceeding with a new color. Designate a separate roller or brush for each color so that you may alternate without having to clean your brush.

3. When all paint is dry, carefully remove the tape at a forty-five-degree angle to prevent the paint from peeling.

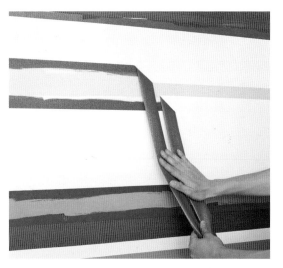

4. To create the thick and thin ticking-stripe effect, continue with a second round of smaller stripes on top of the stripes you've already painted. Repeat steps 1 and 2, starting from outlining the stripes. Note that if you are painting, say, a gray stripe on top of a pink stripe, the pink is your base color, and in step 2 you will paint a second coat of the pink base to help fill in the gaps.

5. Continue the process of adding stripes until the desired design is achieved. Each time the paint of a new stripe is dry, carefully remove the tape at a forty-five-degree angle to prevent the paint from peeling.

6. Voilà! Your stripe accent wall is complete.

FLIRTING WITH
everyday exuberance

By sticking to simple guidelines, this space manages to appear bright and energetic yet calm and collected. The palette is clearly defined—shades of pink and gray repeat and coordinate. No one color stands out prominently or steals center stage. The palette for the painted stripes on the wall was pulled directly from the colors of the furnishings. Additions of white break up the scheme.

FLORAL FUN. This bed illustrates a fully saturated color story. Shades interact directly with one another at essentially the same level of intensity, so they balance each other without any one color dominating. For a change of pace, this duvet cover would also look great paired with a lime green sheet set.

A TAME FLAME. Graphic and bright, this bedding recipe is quite simple: a print duvet and matching shams, solid coverlet, and white sheets with coordinating embroidery. Limiting the palette creates a crisp and happy bedscape. The coordinated orange stripes in the rug make the introduction of green and chocolate welcome in this scheme.

SUNNY-SIDE UP. A single bold pattern can definitively establish a palette for a bedroom. This groovy bed takes the pink, green, and turquoise up a notch with the addition of vivid orange and a touch of buttery yellow. With the balance of the bed in white, the quilt remains absolutely influential.

CHOCOHOLIC. The rich chocolate ground of this duvet cover is the perfect foil for the luscious pink, lemon, and lime crewelwork. The pink hue and the pattern of the daisy-style embroidered flowers are echoed in the shams. Layering it all atop a simple pink and white bed means that a seasonal switch of duvet will be easy.

refined romantic

i like to think we are all romantics at heart

The Refined Romantic style is an invitation to fall in love, to let your heart lead the way. It is a sensibility more than a specific aesthetic. Even die-hard minimalists and modernists can have an appreciation and respect for old-world craftsmanship and the rituals of other times and places. I can't imagine any room that could not benefit from a beautifully carved, gilded antique mirror or a vase bursting with lush roses or peonies.

The goal is not to live in the past or surround oneself with fusty old bits; it's to live with the best the past has to offer. I advocate a restrained approach to romantic style. (I'm allergic to rococo ruffles, porcelain figurines, and anything too frilly or fussy.) The Refined Romantic look is about incorporating beauty, grace, and elegance into a space without a heavy hand—appreciating the allure of a Victorian settee's curves but foregoing the heavy maroon velvet in favor of a light, pearly linen.

In the following pages you will see both modern and traditional Refined Romantic interiors. These include a grand bathroom, a tiny cottage living room, and a sleek but sensual contemporary bedroom—each decidedly Refined Romantic yet possessing very different aesthetics. What they have in common are four key elements:

SHOW YOUR PROVENANCE. (Wrinkles are proof that you have lived!) An object with some age to it, a history or a story to tell, can be incorporated in so many ways to bring romance to a room. It can be as simple as displaying a beloved family photo in a delicate silver frame or using a quilt your great-grandmother made. It can mean buying that circa 1880 farmhouse you fell in love with or being captivated by an antique chair with chipping pink paint and putting it in a very modern room. Find that sentimental part of you and apply it to your interior.

ADD A LITTLE SHINE. Mirrored surfaces and furniture, the glow of candlelight, the glamour of silk, crystal chandeliers, silver-leaf wallpaper—think of using one of the many options as the jewelry in a room, something that catches the light and your eye. Consider an enormous chandelier in a grand ballroom or the unabashed glamour of 1930s Hollywood, when women wore simple satin dresses that shimmered as they sat at their mirrored dressing tables and glistened as they glided down sweeping staircases. Shine is timeless.

SAY IT WITH FLOWERS. Whether you are meandering through a garden lush with roses or have just received a stunning (or not-so-stunning) bouquet from a stunning (or not-so-stunning) man, romance is in the air. Flowers can be found everywhere and on everything, from paintings, china, and needlepoint pillows to wallpaper and fabric.

PAY ATTENTION TO DETAIL. An important element of any romantic interior, details add a rich layer of interest to a room. Think elegant hand painting on a wall or a chest of drawers, or button tufting on a bedroom chair. Once you make a conscious decision to look for detail, you will be able to spot it easily and incorporate it into your rooms, showing that you appreciate the time it took to make an everyday object more beautiful.

A single object, such as an antique sterling silver candlestick with a floral motif, might possess all the Refined Romantic qualities, but most items will hit only one or two of those notes. It's up to you to mix the ingredients in the proportions that seem right for a given room and create a Refined Romantic space that you will love.

refined romantic
fabrics

Take heart! Finding just the right mix of romantic fabrics doesn't have to be daunting. Start by falling in love with a single color or a palette. Refined Romantic is about creating soothing, pretty, sensual spaces, so the colors and fabrics you choose should invite you to look more closely, draw you in, and beg you to touch and admire them. Staying faithful to your palette will help guide you as you encounter what always seems like too many choices.

1. SOFA AND CHAIR UPHOLSTERY. For the largest pieces in the room, I recommend solid-colored or subtly patterned velvet, linen, or other heavier textured fabrics. Keep the larger pieces in one or two colors so the space feels grounded and restful.

2. WINDOW TREATMENTS. Think light, floaty sheers. Cotton organdy, eyelet, and embroidered voile filter the light and soften the edges of a room. They can be used in concert with floor-length curtains in silk, linen, or velvet in a sumptuous solid color.

3. ACCENT UPHOLSTERY. This is where you can have a fling with a more boldly patterned fabric you find irresistible. Use it on a curvy ottoman or a single gilded side chair. I especially like the notion of using attention-getting, elaborate embellished fabrics on modern furniture.

4. DECORATIVE PILLOWS. Exquisite handiwork, beading, embroidery—these are the fabrics that make you gasp when you calculate the effort that went into crafting them. They are perfectly showcased against solid or subtly patterned upholstery.

ELEMENTS OF REFINED ROMANTIC
provenance

As a general rule, good things get better with age. I love pieces with patina—the nicks and dings, the missing or rubbed-off paint that is proof that an object has been well used and well loved. In a modern space, a single, striking piece with some obvious age on it can make a brilliant, bold statement.

AGED FINISHES. Behind every worn edge or chip is a story of storms weathered. The imperfection invites us to feel we can enjoy something without fear of damaging it. Look for wood that has been naturally distressed over time, copper with patina, and gold leaf flaking from wear.

HEIRLOOM LINENS. There is nothing like getting between beautifully pressed, heavy, vintage linen sheets or coming across a quilt someone's great-grandmother slaved over. Estate sales are a great source for such finds. These lovely vintage embroidered shams are favorites of mine.

HAND-ME-DOWNS. It is comforting to include bits of your history in a space. Display a fabulous black-and-white family photograph or opt to use your grandparents' dining table. But remember, you *must* love the piece. If no family heirlooms qualify, hit flea markets, estate sales, antique shops, and websites (1stdibs.com and eBay) for "new" ones that rock your world.

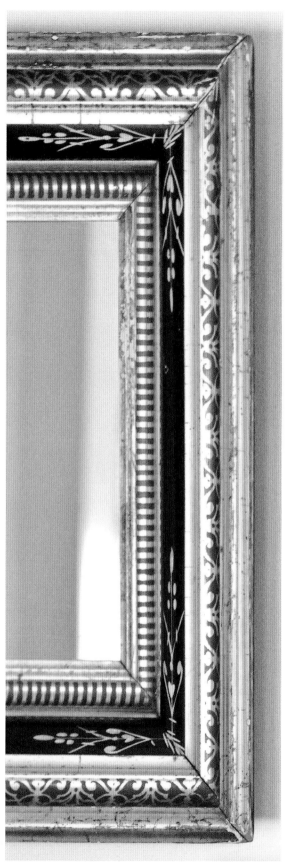

shine

Just as I am attracted to people who have sparkling personalities, I am always drawn to furniture and objects that seem like jewelry for the home.

GILDING. Whether it's a gilded eighteenth-century bergère chair or a delicate gold band on a set of dishes, gilding adds warmth and a touch of grandeur. The key here is a little goes a long way.

POLISHED WOOD. Beautifully polished wood shows grain to its advantage and beckons you to run your hand along its surface. Consider incorporating it in the form of architectural details, furniture, or accent pieces, such as decorative boxes, lamps, and wastebaskets.

CRYSTAL CHANDELIERS AND GLASSWARE. My favorite type of shiny eye candy is a crystal chandelier. I put one up in my linen closet and it makes me happy every time I see it. Crystal and glass accessories lend a refined note to a room.

SILVER. Silver adds a cool, organic sophistication to an interior. Consider silver-leaf mirrors and furniture pieces or smaller touches, such as silver-leaf picture frames, hotel silver, or an antique silver pitcher filled with roses.

MIRRORS AND OTHER REFLECTIVE SURFACES. From a simple wall mirror, mercury glass lamp base, or pair of silver candelabra, to an entirely mirrored chest or wall, reflective surfaces brighten up a dark corner, offer the illusion of added space, and appear magical in candlelight.

flowers

Flowers make you happy! The colors, shapes, and scents always have an uplifting effect.

FRESH FLOWERS. Nothing breathes life and lyricism into a space faster than a delicate flowering branch, a view to a lush, rose-covered garden or a vase overflowing with beautiful blooms.

DECORATED CERAMICS. Use hand-painted ceramics or transferware and look for other ways to display them. Hang a grouping on the wall or use one beautiful saucer as a soap dish.

FABRICS. I think I have seen every possible scale, print, and palette of floral fabric known to man! Find one that makes you swoon and it will continue to bring you happiness for years to come.

WALLPAPER. While many fear committing to a wallpaper, surrounding yourself with subtle or striking flowers can be comforting. I am especially fond of classic, old-fashioned floral wallpaper in a bedroom where the vantage point of the bed allows you to appreciate the intricacy of the design daily.

ARTWORK Think of the restrained sensuality of Mapplethorpe's black-and-white floral photos or ancient Abyssinian stone carvings, 1960s pop-art daisies, or delicate eighteenth-century Chinoiserie panels—there is no wrong period or area of expression. Realistic or abstract, priceless painting or paper posterboard, each floral depiction is wonderful in its own right.

ELEMENTS OF REFINED ROMANTIC
detail

It's the small things—the well-turned leg of a chair, a hand-carved mantel, and the choice of well-mannered accents on a side table—that can have the biggest impact on how a room looks and, more important, how it feels.

SCULPTURAL FURNITURE. I am always drawn to furniture and objects whose form is more lyrical than mundane. Opt for a detailed side chair or a gracefully curved sofa instead of a characterless lump.

ETCHING, ENGRAVING, AND OTHER SURFACE TREATMENTS. Decorations, such as etching on a glass window or champagne glasses, engraving on silver picture frames, or monograms on a sheet or napkin, personalize your items and show extra thoughtfulness.

CARVING. Since the beginning of time, man has left his mark on stone and wood. Carved chairs and tables, lamps, boxes, balusters, jade and marble objects can add old-world distinction.

ARCHITECTURAL DETAIL. If your space is lacking architectural interest, add character with decorative moldings or salvage pieces such as old columns, doors, windows, mantels, and sinks.

DECORATIVE METALWORK. Whether cast or wrought by hand, detailed or gracefully simple, metalwork—gates and grates, doorknobs and knockers, garden furniture, fences and fountains—offers endless inspiration.

dressmaker details

When I was seven years old, my no-nonsense New England mother sent me to take sewing classes with Mrs. Stevens in Stockbridge, Massachusetts. Twice a week after school I would go to her house, where she'd teach me everything she knew about sewing by hand. I continued to study sewing—even in college! But you don't have to know how to sew to appreciate dressmaker details; you just have to recognize them when you see them.

Think of a strikingly simple satin dress draped at the shoulder, falling into soft pleats at the waist. Think of a cascading ruffle on a curtain. Such details turn mere fabric into a seductive statement. These dressmaker details add interest and sophistication to a Refined Romantic interior. I classify them into two categories, architectural detail and adornment.

ARCHITECTURAL DETAIL. Using a needle and thread to create a 3-D form, such as:

- pleating
- ruffles
- pin tucks
- smocking
- button tufting

All of the above are appropriate for window treatments, bed skirts, canopies, and skirts on upholstered pieces.

ADORNMENT. Adding embellishment to the surface of an item that attracts and engages the eye, such as:

- lace edging and other trims
- embroidery
- beading and sequins
- appliqué
- buttons
- gimp
- nailhead trim

These details can be used anywhere, from curtains and pillows to upholstery and slipcovers. The key is not to overdo it. Dressmaker details should enhance the piece they're used on, not overwhelm it.

GIMP: This flat, narrow braid is used to hide the nails necessary to hold upholstery fabric in place. Whether tonal or contrasting, gimp adds a lovely finishing touch.

NAILHEAD TRIM: Evocative of lovely buttons down the back of a fabulous dress, nailhead trim highlights a piece of furniture's curves like a string of beautiful pearls.

LACE BORDERS AND EMBROIDERY: These are the simplest elements to use to add a touch of romance to a room. Use them to trim a pillow, a top sheet, or the edge of a curtain—remembering that a little goes a long way.

RUFFLES AND PLEATS: Ruffles are a bit more feminine, pleats more tailored. I love a one-inch double ruffle or mini pleat as a detail on almost anything, and a three- to four-inch single-sided ruffle or pleat on the edge of a curtain (as here) or a pillow sham.

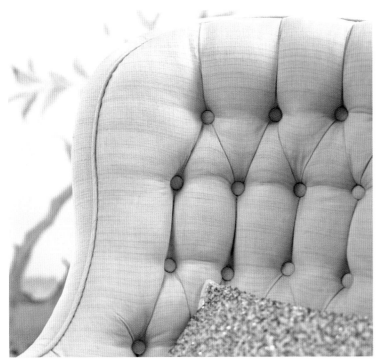

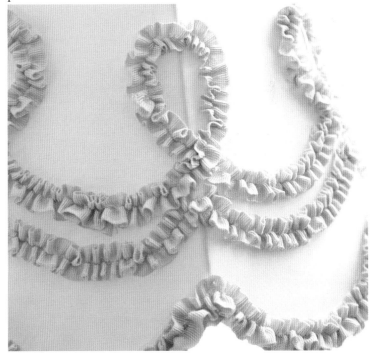

TUFTING: This is an easy way to introduce dressmaker detail to an interior. Think tufting on a Chesterfield sofa, a fabulous sculptural headboard, or an adorable boudoir chair.

RUCHED TRIM: With this sewing technique, fabric or ribbon is gathered pattern to form ruffles, scallops, or petals. This favorite lampshade is made sensational with the simple addition of gathered ribbon. Ruching is also effective on pillows, bedding, and curtains.

a silver lining

When I was dreaming of my new bedroom, I wanted it to be elegant, inviting, and uncluttered, decidedly feminine yet contemporary—a relaxing, uplifting retreat after a long day at work or a grueling business trip (see following pages).

I decided to base the whole design for the room on much-loved panels of hand-painted de Gournay wallpaper that had graced an entire wall in my previous house. I loved the serenity of the weeping willow with its silvery trunk, the lush leaves, and the glamour of the silver-leaf backdrop. It seemed an ideal starting point—a piece with provenance, shine, and detail.

I picked my favorite shade of blue (Farrow & Ball's Pale Powder) for the walls, and then echoed the lightest oyster color of the trunk in the velvet curtains, bed skirt, and tufted headboard. The glam of the silver-leaf ground is echoed in the sensational, modern crystal chandelier. The great ceramic lamps (which I think look like overgrown scallions) pick up the green of the leaves and add another organic element to the space.

In certain parts of the panels, several shades of gray grow almost black. I took a cue from them to add a welcome bit of contrast. When choosing furniture, I looked for dark wood pieces that would anchor the ethereal feel of the room. Ultimately, my bedroom feels like the outdoors brought inside. I find great joy and peace in my silvery, velvety cocoon.

Farrow & Ball
Pale Powder
204

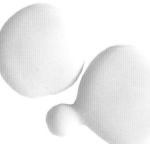

Benjamin Moore
Windy Sky
1638

Benjamin Moore
Dill Pickle
2147-40

NATIONAL MUSEUM OF WOMEN IN THE ARTS

Johannes Vermeer

SEEING OURSELVES: Women's Self-Portraits

PAINTINGS IN THE LOUVRE

isn't she lovely?

I developed the scheme for an adorable cottage living room from the portrait of the lovely lady in the fur-trimmed suit you see here, the very essence of ladylike glamour and refinement. I lifted the room's palette directly from the painting, echoing the fawn of her suit in the oval table and the faux bamboo of the framed mirrors. I used the sable brown fur as inspiration for the long and low cane table piled up with art books. The vivid pink of her lips and the delicate shade of her cheeks spurred my search for vintage fabrics and accessories that incorporated these rosy hues.

The elongated mirrors make the room appear larger, add sparkle, and help to flood the space with reflected daylight. Gilt frames and the gilded floral motif on the pink vase keep the shimmer moving around the room. Detail is found in the delicate hand-painted mural on the back wall and in the band of nickel nailhead trim surrounding the base of each sofa. The element of provenance comes from the lovely antique cane bed adapted for use as a table, the great and unusually pretty antique Oriental rug, and the eighteenth- and nineteenth-century floral fabrics I chose for the pillows on the sofas.

Fresh-cut flowers—peonies, hydrangeas, and Queen Anne's lace— abound. The four elements work in concert to invite you to sit right down, open a book, and spend an afternoon enjoying the amazing *Paintings of the Louvre.*

a new flame

The big room that follows needed some warming up. When I fell head over heels for this unusually beautiful rug, I knew I had found my muse. This was not a match made in heaven, however. The room required a much larger floor covering, but instead of searching for something more "size-appropriate," I was determined to find another rug to use alongside the one I had already given my heart to.

I studied my beloved rug, trying to identify what about it so spoke to me. I decided it was the combination and balance of colors and the graphic yet delicate patterns. This established my palette, and then the room started to take shape in my mind.

I was thrilled to find a Farrow & Ball wallpaper in just the right shade of terra-cotta. It instantly conferred an understated, earthy quality to the room. The color seems to warm you from the inside out. I discovered the ivory ground paisley fabric on a trip to India and had it quilted, a detail that made the overstuffed chairs even more inviting. The lovely greeny-blue from the rug is mirrored in the tactile and durable cotton velvet on the long Chesterfield sofa. Adding some favorite watercolors of my mother's and the lovely drum table from my grandmother made the room feel complete.

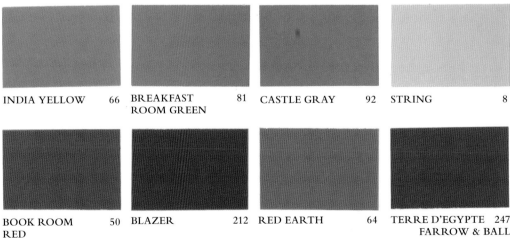

| INDIA YELLOW | 66 | BREAKFAST ROOM GREEN | 81 | CASTLE GRAY | 92 | STRING | 8 |
| BOOK ROOM RED | 50 | BLAZER | 212 | RED EARTH | 64 | TERRE D'EGYPTE FARROW & BALL | 247 |

gold crush

This stunningly decorated English manor house ceiling shown at far left was the inspiration for the following beautiful bedroom. The balance of white, pale pink, and shades of dove gray creates the perfect backdrop for the restrained gilding. Just as jewelry should be chosen to enhance and not overwhelm an ensemble, the use of gold in this room is just right. I wanted the room to feel similarly feminine but not sickly sweet, regal but not imposing.

I also wanted the showstopper bed to be a focal point, but I balanced its bling with subtle grays and whites. I started by painting the walls pale gray, then added sheer linen floor-to-ceiling curtains to diffuse the light and add a fluid softness to the wall of windows. The gray demilune bedside tables are strong enough to anchor but not compete with the bed, and the solid pale pink and white bed linens keep your eye focused on the bed's tracery. The dish of roses adds the perfect touch of pink to this elegant scheme.

Benjamin Moore
Cloud White
OC-130

Benjamin Moore
Timid White
OC-39

Benjamin Moore
Pismo Dunes
AC-32

Benjamin Moore
Pink Peony
2078-70

Gold Leaf

mounded roses

1. Using a damp rag, remove the thorns and leaves from each rose stem and any unwanted or bruised petals.

2. Using a good pair of floral shears, trim the end of each stem underwater. This will lengthen the life of the bloom by preventing air from traveling up the stem.

3. To begin mounding the roses, group the first four buds, then carefully rotate and add more stems evenly around. Hold them firmly to prevent slipping.

4. When you are finished, use floral tape to secure the bouquet about four inches below the bottom of the blooms.

5. Measure the ends of the stems against the vase you will be using, to determine where to cut the stems. Cut them underwater to the desired length. *Note: Start longer and then trim, to avoid cutting off too much length.*

6. Place the bouquet in the vase with water. Use a floral food additive to extend the life of the arrangement. The roses will open up, so expect the bouquet to fill out over the course of the day.

FLIRTING WITH
refined romantic

Intrigued but not quite ready to take the plunge? Start with a small area such as an entryway (as shown here), bathroom, or dining table. There is nothing particularly romantic about this backdrop, a simple off-white wall with a touch of beadboard. It is through the introduction of Refined Romantic elements that the style comes to life.

SHINE: the mirror, silver vase, and votive holders. The mirror reflects the votives, giving a warm, inviting aura to the space.

DETAIL: the carving on the Louis Philippe–style mirror, the curvy hardware, and the white painted detail framing the drawers on the chest.

PROVENANCE: the chest, mirror, and multi-arm plant stand. All are vintage, collected from various sources, including Brimfield, eBay, and a local thrift store.

FLOWERS: the individual arrangements of mounded creamy white roses. Set in a variety of vessels, including porcelain cups, bowls, and silver vases, the groups of blooms give the vignette its final romantic flourish. A single arrangement in a tall vase would have worked well as a less elaborate option.

HOW-TO: dressing the refined romantic bed

AM I BLUE? This two-tone bed is refined and feminine, featuring dressmaker details such as scallops, ruffles, and lyrical embroidery. The hand-crocheted coverlet lends provenance, while the meandering floral is restful. The two-color palette allows interplay of the floral and stripe without detracting from the overall peaceful feeling of the bed.

SHEER HEAVEN. Like a fabulous wedding dress, this bed is sophisticated, updated, and utterly feminine without being frilly or fussy. The mirror-work embroidered pillow not only provides an element of shine but also adds texture and pattern to the otherwise white bed.

A WARM EMBRACE. This bed has many exquisite details, but no one dominates. The intricate quilt, the delicate ruched trim on the sheeting, and the pleats on the skirt, duvet, and shams are all in balance. The simplicity of solids makes the vintage pillow all the more delightful. The rougher texture and neutral color of the linen accessories tempers the pink.

FEATHER YOUR NEST. The printed duvet cover was adapted from a favorite nineteenth-century document print in my collection. I love the palette, particularly for a bedroom—varying shades of blue, aqua, and platinum. The print speaks for itself; however, the tiny ruffle on the sheet adds just the right amount of delicacy to the bed.

happy preppy

find the fun in functional

Enjoying the elemental pleasures of life—spending time with family and friends, communing with nature, walking, sailing, swimming, fishing—is the foundation on which Happy Preppy style is built. This quintessentially American look embraces the spirited characteristics of an active life and the practical side of time-honored tradition.

Happy Preppy rooms possess a no-nonsense, happy-go-lucky quality that makes them livable and lovable.

These rooms are places where anyone can feel at home, where people still work on jigsaw puzzles and play backgammon in front of the fireplace, where you'll find reading lamps next to every chair and a table for a cocktail or a cup of tea. Sports equipment is at the ready for the next adventure. In these pet- and kid-friendly environments you can feel free to put your feet up and truly relax. No pieces are so precious that a bit of dog slobber (a topic on which I'm an expert) will cause a meltdown.

This look isn't difficult to achieve because the building blocks are the basics. You start by finding honest-to-goodness, practical, classic pieces of furniture, old or new. Limit your palette to the cheerful Crayola colors of childhood; these are the sporty, energetic hues that stand out on race cars, team uniforms, or a classic yellow rain slicker. Then choose workhorse fabrics that wash well and stand up to use. Focusing on the following four elements will get you most of the way to happy preppiness:

YOU CAN NEVER GO WRONG WITH A CLASSIC. This goes for coffee tables as well as clothes. These are pieces that have stood the test of time, that were so well conceived they've never been replaced. They do the job and look good doing it. These are the pieces you should crack open your piggy bank to buy. Look for the best possible quality, because you can rest assured that they will never go out of style.

UTILITY CANNOT BE OVERRATED. This is about prioritizing functionality. It means celebrating the useful, everyday objects that make your life easier, objects that do the job for which they were intended. Not surprisingly, many wonderfully functional pieces become classics.

ADD A DASH OF PEP. This means introducing lively tidbits to the room that convey energy and enthusiasm. Include something silly or sentimental, something that makes you smile. It is the sharing of these personal pleasures that makes everyone feel welcome and relaxed.

PACK A GRAPHIC PUNCH. The elements can take many forms, as in a bold wall of color or the striking use of pattern, such as stripes, checks, or dots. Try hanging vintage signs as art. The key is simply to punctuate your place with pops of color to increase visual interest.

Happy Preppy embraces the belief that less is more. That means keeping it simple yet stylish, functional but fun. While this way of living has its roots in the country and by the water, this style can be a welcome retreat from the daily grind of urban life as well. Even on a gray city day, in a Happy Preppy home the sun is always shining.

happy preppy
fabrics

Don't overthink it. Limit your palette to mainly primary colors, which will ensure graphic punch. Look for fabrics that are rough-and-tumble (as in no fuss, tumble dry)—this is not a dry-clean-only world! Choose fabrics with a history of durable service; you'll appreciate the can-do, never-say-die spirit that seems to be woven right into the cloth. As an added bonus, these workhorse fabrics are among the least expensive on the market, so you can invest your money in classic pieces of furniture instead.

LARGER UPHOLSTERED PIECES. Keep it simple by choosing a sturdy cotton duck in white or ivory, a denim in any wash that appeals, or a toothy brushed twill in khaki, white, ivory, or red.

ACCENT UPHOLSTERY. Choose a textured solid in your favorite shade of red, green, yellow, or blue to add a pop of color. An especially bright solid—a single splash of bright green or chipper yellow on a chair or an ottoman—can instantly bring a room to life.

WINDOW TREATMENTS. I prefer something tailored and unfussy, such as solid white or off-white panels or Roman shades. They can be left plain or enhanced with a simple binding in a contrasting color that matches the accent upholstery. If you feel daring, bold primary stripes or checks can be very effective. For a lighter look, which works best in bedrooms and bathrooms, consider white organdy sheers, seersucker, or shirting stripes.

DECORATIVE ACCESSORIES. Here's where you can get your yayas out at last: with decorative pillows, napkins, or tablecloths. Go crazy with prints—dots, stripes, and blocky florals—the more the merrier. The trick to success is to stay within the bright palette of primary colors. Continuity of color makes it work. Stay graphic with two-tone or color-blocked multi prints.

ELEMENTS OF HAPPY PREPPY
classic

Classics aren't born; it's through years of reliable service that classics emerge, becoming definitive, go-to pieces, often for generations. They weather trend after trend and still come out on top. The designs are so well conceived, so well executed from the get-go that there is no improvement necessary.

UPHOLSTERY. Invest in pieces and shapes that don't date, such as Tuxedo, Bridgewater, and track arm style sofas. Look for kiln-dried frames with eight-way hand-tied springing. Then look for a good slipcover person! My mother invested in a well-made, classic sofa thirty-five years ago. It has lived in three different houses and has had six different slipcovers. It has never looked dated. It did require a transfusion of down into the cushions sometime in the early '90s, but this is a never-say-die piece that will last for decades to come.

OTHER FURNITURE. Vintage stores and flea markets are fabulous sources for affordable furniture. I look for beautiful, solidly built pieces in classic shapes that have a gently worn appeal or that can be refinished or freshened up with a coat of paint. Usually built out of sturdy hardwood, pieces made before the advent of MDF (medium-density fiberboard) are a great bet.

FLOORING. Quarter-sawn oak planks, linoleum, cork, one- or two-inch hexagonal marble tile, wool, sisal, or Axminster-style carpets—these are all classic choices underfoot.

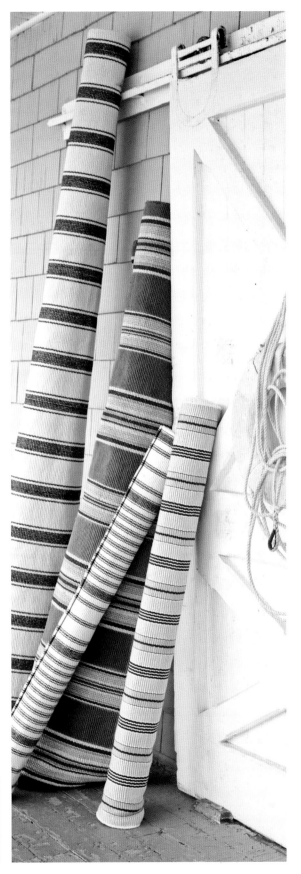

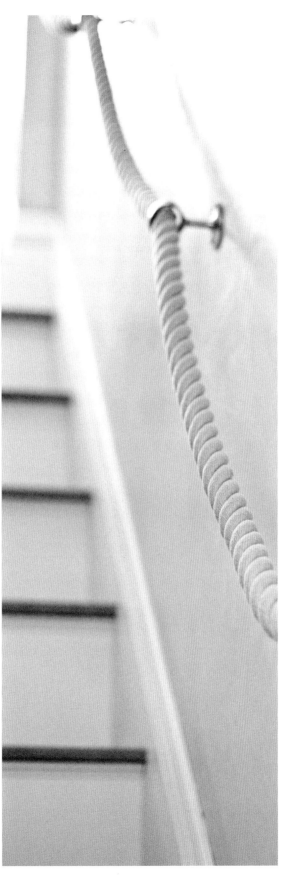

utility

Isn't it lovely when things work as they were intended? No fuss, no muss, just plain old-fashioned functionality. These items do the job you need them to do. Attractive in an honest, understated way, they are thus welcome additions to our lives and an essential part of the Happy Preppy look.

These pages show a varied cross section of items that all share the quality of being especially useful:

INVEST IN ITEMS YOU USE EVERY DAY. These little functional luxuries are worth their weight in gold:

- Sturdy, serviceable hardware and appliances for your kitchen and bathrooms

- Good knives and finger-friendly cabinet hardware

- A showerhead that makes you happy every day

KEEP IT CLEAN. Spend less time cleaning and more time doing things you love:

- Keep dirt from entering the house, with doormats and boot scrapers.

- Invest in easy-to-clean household objects such as indoor/outdoor rugs and fabrics, linoleum and tile flooring, and washable slipcovers for furniture.

GO GREEN. Look for products that do the job but don't adversely affect our environment, such as clotheslines and cloth napkins, and roller towels.

pep

Pep is what puts the *happy* in *Happy Preppy*. A strictly preppy approach could seem fusty, controlled, and uptight. But Happy Preppy embraces the lighter, perkier side of tradition and invites you to insert your own brand of enthusiasm into the mix.

1. Add a brightly colored modern chair to a traditional space.

2. Try sunny vintage tableware and linens or a bouquet of daffodils in an unexpected vessel.

3. Display a quirky object—such as the dolphin at right—that makes you smile. This dolphin, found at Brimfield after being retired from a water park, has made surprise appearances in various locations in my house, greeting guests on occasion at the door, and once even stealing the show as the centerpiece for a dinner party.

4. Put a yellow rubber duck on the edge of the tub—even if you don't have any children in the house.

Embrace optimism. Let your hair down and show the world your silly side. Most of all, have some fun. My prep school roommate used to say, "We are here for a good time, not a long time." Identify and celebrate the things that make you happy, and put them on display.

graphic

Think of strongly defined objects or treatments that instantly draw your eye and add impact and energy to a space. Look for items that show up vividly against their background. Go for anything that grabs your eye.

TEXTILES. Stripes, plaids, and checks are a crisp, timeless way to add punch to windows, upholstery, bedding, towels, and rugs. Look for crisp, bold, or larger-scale versions, as smaller scales don't offer much in the impact department.

GRAPHIC IMPACT. Consider the effect an individual piece will have: a red chair against a white wall, for instance, or, even more fun, a white chair against a vivid red wall. In addition to contrasts of color, the shapes of furniture and objects can add to a sense of graphic impact.

EVERYDAY OBJECTS. Look for pieces that provide an affordable way to add splashes of striking, solid color to a room—brightly colored laundry baskets, storage totes, plastic glasses, napkins, pillows, alarm clocks, and picture frames.

COLOR BLOCKING WITH PAINT. Try channeling Ellsworth Kelly and create impact on your wall with paint. Tape off a series of squares and fill them with happy, Crayola-inspired colors.

ARTWORK. Look for bold, clearly defined imagery in any medium from photography to your children's tempera paintings, from abstract oil painting to posters, vintage signs, and lettering. You do not want subtle; you want sensational.

happy preppy palette

Just as these signal flags stand out and are easily "read" from long distances, think graphic, bold, and simple when considering a palette for a Happy Preppy space. This is above all a practical look imbued with energy. Reflecting and drawing from an active, athletic tradition, the palette should be confident and clear, simple and easily recognized, like the colors of your favorite sports team.

Use color as punctuation throughout a room, and combine it with copious amounts of white or natural wood. Keep it simple. When it comes to paint, white and off-white cannot be overused. They make any space look bigger and brighter instantly.

If you are looking for something more dramatic, try a saturated color on the walls and highlight it with white trim. You might try a single wide horizontal stripe moving around a room, or vertical stripes at regular intervals. This allows you to add graphic pattern to a wall without the hassle of searching for and then hanging wallpaper.

1. Benjamin Moore Utah Sky

2. Behr Shamrock

3. Sherwin-Williams Real Red

4. Benjamin Moore Timid White

5. Sherwin-Williams Derbyshire

6. Benjamin Moore Tequila Lime

7. Benjamin Moore Decorators White

8. Benjamin Moore Blue Lapis

9. Sherwin-Williams Cheerful

10. Benjamin Moore Sparkling Sun

11. Benjamin Moore Heritage Red

12. Behr Midnight Dream

13. Behr Handsome Hue

14. Sherwin-Williams Frank Blue

15. Benjamin Moore Caribbean Coast

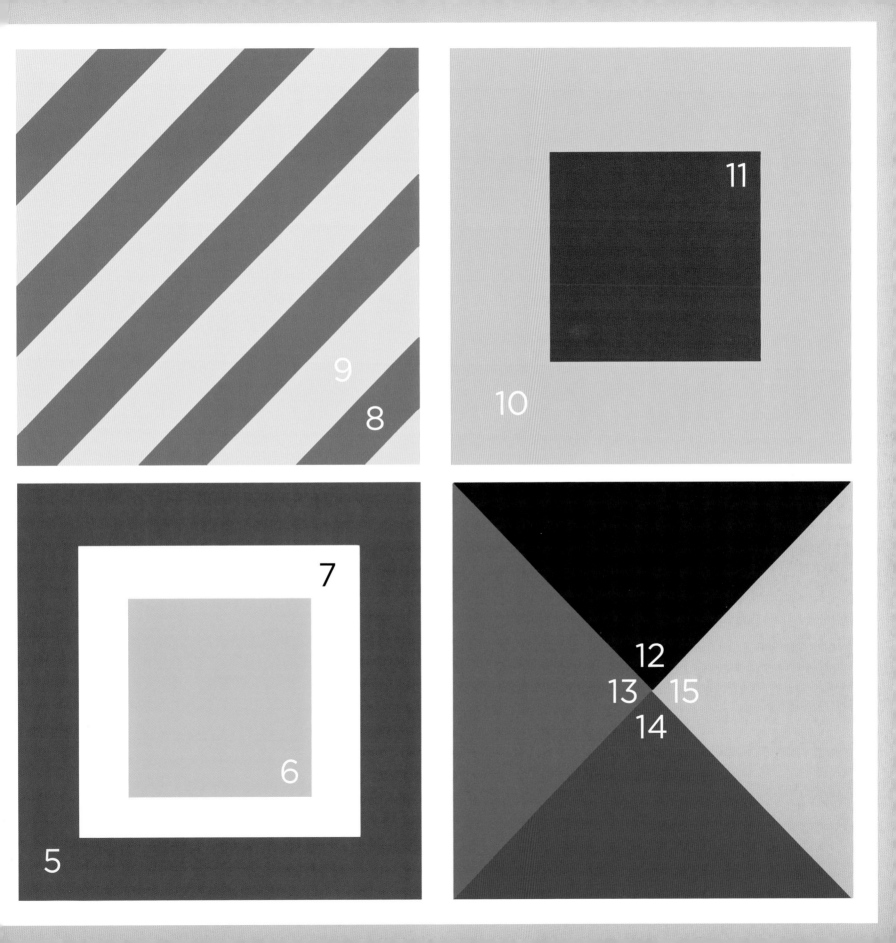

happy preppy details

1. GET HAPPY AT THE HARDWARE STORE. Your local hardware store can be a great place to find attractive and reasonably priced pieces that can be cleverly repurposed to add functionality and an authentic flair to Happy Preppy spaces. Far less expensive than rings sold as "decorative curtain hardware," the O-rings pictured here are conveniently offered in brass or chrome finishes, and the snap clip is used to create a functionally fashionable curtain tieback.

2. TRIED-AND-TRUE TRIMS. Rickrack, seam binding, and plain old grosgrain ribbon can add zip to lampshades, curtains and curtain tiebacks, Roman shades, sheets, pillowcases, and towels. A small touch of color offers variety and can tie items in a scheme together. Trim can be a particularly effective way of making off-the-shelf basics look like they were custom-made for the space.

3. ATTENTION TO DETAIL. There is a fine line between utterly functional and dull. Happy Preppy is clean and uncluttered, so there are no grand gestures like droopy fringes to distract the eye. Instead, simple tailoring techniques add crispness and distinction. For example, adding a self-bias trim to this tattersall pillow sham is subtle and shows attention to detail. Make solid pillows and uphol-stery sing by adding a contrast welt in a color that matches another shade used in your space. Create graphic impact on pillows, cur-tains, or bedding by using simple patchwork techniques, as seen in the two-tone pillow. This is a way of working with inexpensive fabrics to create a strong visual impact.

4. MONOGRAMS. Used sparingly, monograms can be an effective way to personalize and add a pop of color to pillows, coverlets, headboards, shower curtains, and linens. Don't overdo it. A little goes a long way!

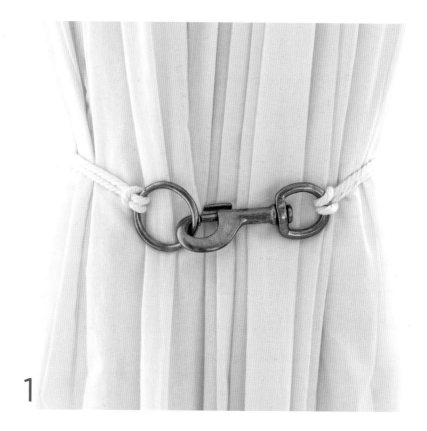

1

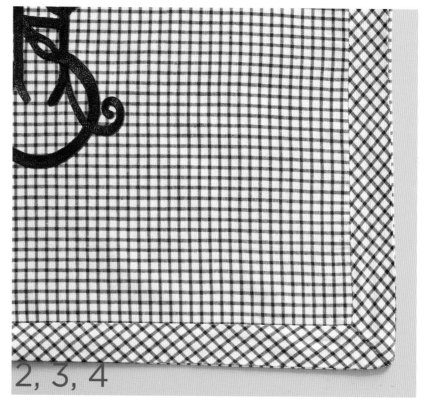

2, 3, 4

1

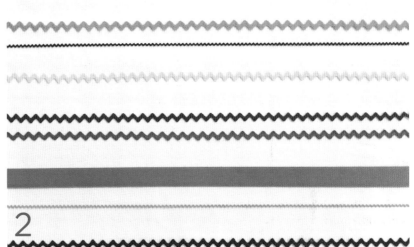

2

3

3

shipshape

Surrounded by the boats that inspired the design, and guided by the straightforward functionality found in a ship's cabin, the room that follows is purposely uncluttered. Sticking to a simple blue-and-white scheme offers the opportunity to use a variety of stripes and patterns in various shades of blue without creating visual overload. A straight blue-and-white palette can often feel cold, but here the natural wood on the floor and ceiling provides a warmer, more inviting atmosphere.

The striking rug adds visual energy to the space. The fact that it is indoor/outdoor and cleaned in a jiffy earns it high marks for utility, too. Intriguingly shaped, the lamps are fun yet full-on functional.

Classic elements include ticking on the wing chair and beadboard on the ceiling. The Shaker-style bed, the focal point of the room, is primarily classic as well, dressed in tailored hotel-style bedding. A bit of graphic zip and a touch of whimsy are found in the patchwork coverlet made from vintage bandanas folded across the foot.

a sunny disposition

The delightful living room on the next spread defies the possibility of ever having a bad day. You can practically feel the happiness emanating from every inch of the space. The best news is that this is an exceptionally simple room recipe. The plaster walls are lightly tinted with a warming touch of pink. The trim is painted in a crisp white semi-gloss for subtle contrast. White duck slipcovers on the sofa and equally practical Sunbrella on the chairs mean fabulously family-friendly, unfussy upholstery.

When the major components of the room are utterly neutral, they become a remarkably blank canvas for the punches of graphic color that keep your eye moving around the room. Kids' artwork, a pair of contemporary watercolors, a punchy pennant collage, and vivid pillows on the relaxed and squishy sofa make the space at once perky and pleasing, beckoning you and your muddy dogs and ice-cream-covered children to put your feet up and dive into a good book or play a board game. A classic cotton ticking rug in a bright blue connects many of the decorative elements and adds a crisp focal point to the room. The capacious tray table holds all the books, magazines, games, and drinks you'll need for a relaxed and fun-filled gathering.

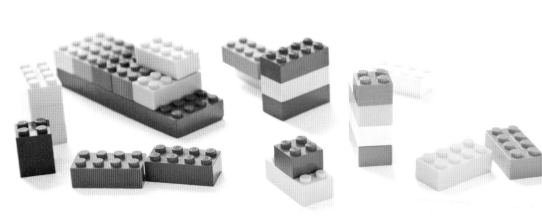

red, light, and blue

Fresh and unfussy, the summer lunch scheme that follows is an easy foray into Happy Preppy style. Anchored by a classic teak table and chairs, the whole scene gets revved up with the addition of graphic red-and-white print cushions and a blue-and-white indoor/outdoor rug in a time-honored ticking stripe. Serving pieces, the familiar disposable plastic cups, fresh strawberries presented in a utilitarian yet attractive colander, and the sprightly geraniums echo the red and blue. Touches of yellow and copious flashes of green keep the scheme from becoming monotonous.

There is little question that red, white, and blue is a compelling, all-American combination. But when adopting this classic palette for decorating, I urge you to move past the patently patriotic and find an arrangement that captures the impact and energy these colors create. Each primary color here is used on its own or paired with white or off-white. Avoid prints or patterns that have red, white, and blue all together.

parlor games

What makes the following family-friendly living room successful is the practically palpable energy of centuries clashing. Mid-century modern furniture and accessories rub elbows with architecture of the 1800s. Classically country elements, such as the intricately patched antique star quilt, are reinvigorated when juxtaposed with the classically modern Arco lamp, angular chairs, and coffee table.

The space appears crisp yet welcoming, and homey without being schmaltzy or cloying. I'd call it country with a modern edge. The grand scale coffee table is an anchor big enough to accommodate a game of Monopoly, the Sunday *Times,* and plenty of people around it. The sofa, slipcovered in wonderfully washable denim, looks more downtown than down home.

Displayed as art, the quilt's game-board-hued palette unifies the seemingly disparate colors such as the Crayola-green leather and happy red lacquered chairs.

HOW-TO: adding racing stripes to towels

1. Completely open the binding and place the back side of the towel against the front side of the binding, lining up the edges. Stitch them together in the crease of the binding closest to the edges of the towel and binding.

2. Turn over the towel, folding the binding over so the center crease aligns with the edge of the towel. Stitch along the bottom of the binding.

3. Cut any excess binding on the towel's edge, leaving no material on either end.

4. Repeat steps 1, 2, and 3 on the parallel edge of the towel.

5. For both remaining sides, repeat step 1, leaving one extra inch of binding on both ends of the towel. Turn the towel over and, with the binding open, fold the extra inch of binding over the corners on each side of the towel and then fold over the towel's top edge, in order to finish the corners of the towel.

6. Stitch along the bottom of the binding as you did in step 2 for the first two sides.

FLIRTING WITH
happy preppy

Limiting the palette to a two-tone scheme takes a guest bath from basic to brilliant. The Happy Preppy bases are all covered in this quick-fix bathroom. The classic white beadboard backdrop is invigorated through color coordination. This red is perky, but the room would be equally effective in any sassy shade you chose. Sticking to the one color allows the pieces to work in harmony and pack a graphic punch. The vintage towel bar with glass shelf is elegant. Adding the racing stripe to a plain white towel provides the finishing pep.

dressing the happy preppy bed

COLOR BLOCKING AND COLOR COORDINATION. This crisp, tailored bedscape's bold impression is simple to pull off. The impact comes from using strong blocks of color—a zesty green balanced by blocks of white. The coordinating green stripes in the decorative pillows make the introduction of blues work nicely on this bed.

WASHABLE, WEARABLE, WONDERFUL. Like a great pair of jeans with a striped linen shirt, this bed has an off-the-cuff, relaxed elegance. Straightforward pieces in classic cotton and linen blend effortlessly and feel at home anywhere. Also, like your favorite jeans, the textiles on this no-fuss bed only get better with age.

MAKING A STATEMENT. This fabulous pattern brings instant graphic pizzazz to any room. Keeping the rest of the bed quiet and beautifully tailored means the print takes center stage. Duvet covers can be changed out as often as you want; look for eye-popping patterns that bring you happiness, then layer the bed with all-white pieces.

UPDATED TRADITION. This quilt is graphic but not granny, basic but not boring. Dig in your attic for a classic quilt that has some zip. (Note: buying new is also totally acceptable.) Then pick up one or more of the colors in it as accent pillows and you've got a classic, graphic bed with an updated yet familiar, comfortable feel.

nuanced neutral

neutral is anything but colorless!

As funny as it seems, I think there are actually more color considerations in a neutral palette than a multi-hued scheme. With a restrained palette, each object or color is thrown into relief and you become much more aware of the distinctions, subtle though they may be. I have often said there is nothing duller than a "beige for beige's sake" interior, where someone chose to play it totally, blandly safe. But when the nuances within the neutral palette are explored, mixed, and layered, exciting depth and intrigue emerge in the space. If a neutral room is crafted with focus, it can evoke both exuberance and calm.

Neutral rooms can be traditional or modern, romantic or formal. They can be crisp and tailored, or monastic and minimalistic. They can be low-key or lively; bright and light or brooding and moody. There are many possibilities for creating a very individualistic space; however, I believe the most successful neutral interiors, regardless of style, incorporate the same basic elements.

CONSIDER SHAPE. Select pieces with interesting silhouettes. Aim for a mix of curvaceous and straight-edged, angular and flowing, round and square.

TAKE ON TEXTURE. When you start to really look at objects, building materials, fabrics, or artwork, notice the variations of texture. Seek to juxtapose multiple types of textiles such as matte, shiny, nubby, smooth, hard, soft, and so on. The mix makes each stand out.

BRING NATURE IN. Every interior benefits from an infusion of nature. For the neutral palette in particular, natural elements are a part of the design. Perhaps this is because nature also provides endless inspiration for neutral interiors. Look, for instance, at the speckles on a quail's egg or the bark of a tree and you will find that you can extract a perfectly balanced neutral palette.

LAYER AWAY. Once you are comfortable with the concepts of shape, texture, and nature, it's time to experiment with layering these elements. Think of the room as a blank canvas and each addition to it as another brushstroke: the wall color, the flooring type, the fabrics, and the furniture. The beauty of a neutral palette is that objects in the palette tend to play well together, so you can move them around and combine them in a number of different ways.

The rooms that follow have much to offer in the way of inspiration. They come from multiple spaces in two very different houses, creations of friends who are artful practitioners of the Nuanced Neutral aesthetic. My friend Jane's house is a white clapboard colonial dating to 1833, while the Copper House, home to architects Peter Franck and Kathleen Triem, is unwaveringly modern. Both settings are living, breathing family homes, complete with kids, dogs, cats, and the stuff of life. Yet each exudes a timeless, nuanced sophistication.

1, 4

1, 2

2

1, 2

1, 2

1, 3

2, 3

2, 3

3

nuanced neutral
fabrics

People are often lulled into a false sense of "I can't make a mistake if I stay neutral." Unfortunately this isn't really the case. It's important to choose fabrics in a range of tones and textures; this variety is what adds the *nuanced* to *neutral*. Because there are so many fabrics to choose from, however, it's extremely helpful to have an idea of what sensibility you are looking to achieve before you start shopping. The key is first to establish a palette, and then see it through with a variety and combination of weights and textures.

Study neutral rooms that please you in houses you visit, in this book, and in magazines. Take photos, tear out or photocopy pages—whatever will help you keep track of the interiors you love. Look closely at the combination of fabrics. Note the patterns you are most drawn to and ask yourself why. Explore the degrees between warm and cool, light and dark, and smooth and rough. Play with various options until you find a balance of multiple colors and textures that reflects your vision. It's the differences that elevate a selection from boring to brilliant.

Illustrated here are a beach-inspired, warm neutral palette and on the following spread a cool neutral palette derived from rocks. Notice that the warm palette ranges from ivory to chocolate, and the cool palette from white to black—there are endless variations within each spectrum. Here are some suggested uses for the fabrics shown:

1. UPHOLSTERY

2. WINDOWS

3. ACCENT UPHOLSTERY AND DECORATIVE PILLOWS

4. SLIPCOVERS

1, 2

2

2

2, 4

1, 2, 3

4

2

2, 4

1, 4

1, 2, 3, 4

1, 3, 4

shape

Shape is essential for creating an inviting Nuanced Neutral space, because you don't have the wow factor of color or pattern on which to rely. Shapes stand out against a neutral ground, and the sculptural appeal of a well-chosen vase, a curvaceous chair, or a light fixture can elevate objects to functional art. When choosing objects consider their contour, silhouette, and visual appeal as shapes:

1. Notice whether an object is symmetrical or asymmetrical, curvaceous or angular.

2. Take note of the characteristics and combinations of shapes that appeal to you. Sofas and chairs can be sensual and curvy or trim and tailored. Cocktail tables and end tables can be angular or graceful.

3. Consider the sculptural impact an object will have on the room. Does the object have visual presence?

To arrange the objects you have chosen for maximum impact:

1. Leave enough space around the object so that its contour can be appreciated.

2. If the object is dark, position it against a lighter backdrop for contrast, and vice versa if it is light. For instance, if you have dark floors and a dark coffee table, try adding a lighter rug so the lines of the table will be shown to their best advantage.

3. Remember not to cram too many shapely pieces together. Balance the mix of shapes in the room.

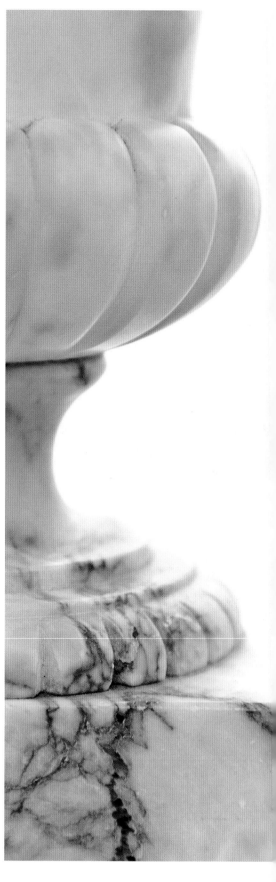

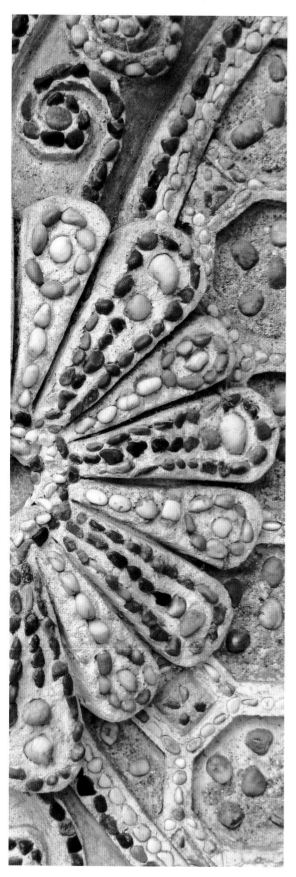

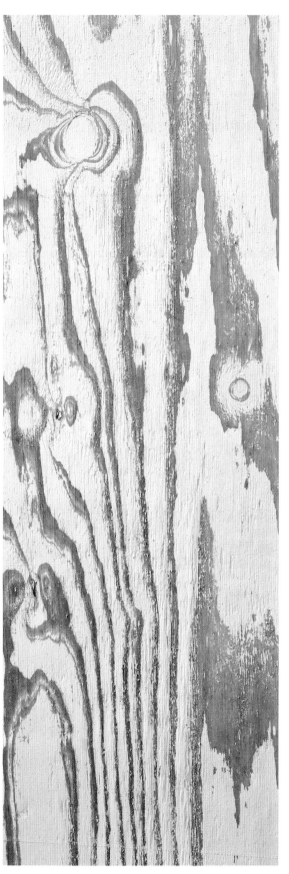

texture

Everything has texture, both visual and tactile, and every surface reflects light differently. Look for variety. Imagine a space in which every surface—walls, countertops, floors—was shiny. It would be visually overwhelming because all parts of the room would be reflecting light at the same high intensity. By contrast, using matte-finish paint on the walls, wood on the countertops, and a rough stone for the floor creates a textural range with depth and balance, as each surface absorbs and reflects light differently.

Whether you are building new, redoing an existing space, or just sprucing up an interior, make decisions about the walls and floors first, since they are the largest surfaces in the space. Next, look for furniture, textiles, objects, and accessories that vary in texture and play them off one another.

The following are broad categories of textures and a few of their infinite variations:

SMOOTH. Ceramic, plastic, painted wood, leather

ROUGH. Raw stone, hewn plank wood, rusted metal, bark

SOFT. Textiles, fur, carpet, rugs

HARD. Metal, wood, stone

MATTE. Plaster, flat paint, honed stone surfaces, paper, ceramic

GLOSSY. Glass, polished stone, stainless steel, chrome, patent leather

nature

Nature provides endless inspiration, teaches so many lessons (both profound and practical), and supplies us with the most diverse and intriguing building materials you could ever ask for. Elements from the outdoors ground a space and add a welcome note of imperfection.

WOOD. With its myriad grains, hues, and textures, wood adds warmth and depth to a room. I think wood works best when it is offset by other materials that highlight its unique qualities.

STONE. Stone intrinsically conveys a sense of timelessness and strength. Choices for stone flooring and wall tile range from shiny or tumbled marble, slate, bluestone, and limestone, to mosaic. Tables and countertops are another great use for stone. Accessories such as vessels, sculpture, and architectural salvage offer a less permanent option for adding the qualities of stone.

ORGANIC MATTER. Bringing pieces of nature inside is another way of adding diversity of texture and form. Birch bark, river rocks, coral, shells, pinecones—really anything that strikes your fancy—all bring a special presence to any space. I often gather pieces during my dog walks in the woods.

PLANT LIFE. The quickest and simplest way to introduce nature into your space is to add a living—and yes, breathing—plant. Ferns, cacti, *Schefflera*—any potted plant is a welcome addition. Consider the vessel in which it lives. Don't let it detract from the plant.

layer

The artful layering of surfaces, shapes, and colors is the foundation of a successful Nuanced Neutral interior. Layering may not be immediately apparent, because when it's done well, it is nearly imperceptible. It simply makes you want to go back and look at the space again and again.

BREAKING IT DOWN

SHAPE. Consider the room's architecture, the contour of pieces of furniture, the line of lamps, artwork, and accessories. For instance, notice the pronounced layers of shape in the ceramic vases (opposite)—taller and shorter, fatter and skinnier, and then very subtle layers of color, in the four shades of white. The glossy texture acts as a constant.

COLOR: Ask yourself: How does the color of this object relate to the colors of the other pieces? Does the object stand out against its backdrop or is it lost? The difference can be very subtle or dramatic, but there should always be some point of differentiation. The table setting (opposite), contains many different layers, clearly showing how the pieces, stacked one atop the other, expand and enrich the overall palette.

TEXTURE: Are you including enough different textures to keep the eye moving around the room? Are you spanning the range of shiny to matte, rough to smooth? Notice the range of textures in the image to the immediate left—from highly polished wood to matte ceramic to a chenille and nubby ivory textured fabrics.

PUTTING IT TOGETHER

Understanding layering is pretty simple, but learning how to put it into practice takes some time. It requires trial and error to strike the right balance. Compiling samples or swatches of all the components of a room—flooring, carpet, tile, fabrics, wallpaper (opposite)— helps you get an idea of how the various parts of the puzzle will come together. Play with them, adding and subtracting and using bigger and smaller bits to determine the best combinations and proportions of each for the room.

paint details

There are countless neutral paints, ranging from the brightest white to the deepest chocolate. Where do you start? Here you will find some of my favorites in the pastel, mid, and deep tones. When choosing paints, keep in mind the following:

WHITES. Every white has a tinge of color. The easiest way to understand this is to look at a group of "white" paint chips. This highlights the subtle or quite pronounced differences among shades of white. Farrow & Ball's Dimity (#13) has a pink tinge, whereas their Blackened (#10) has a purply-blue tint. Before settling on a paint color, think about what you want to achieve. Are you looking for cool or warm, bright or subtle? This simple step will help you sort through myriad options.

MID TONES. The addition of pigment to paint highlights the warm or cool differences in color. Whites and mid tones create most of the layering of palette in a nuanced neutral room.

DEEPS. I look for a lively deep to complete the range in a neutral space. To me this means it must have a hint of a color outside the neutral range. Browns often have a hint of red, green, or yellow that lends more warmth and depth than black, which usually has a flatter look.

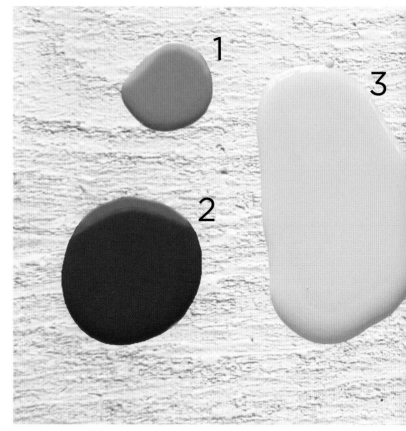

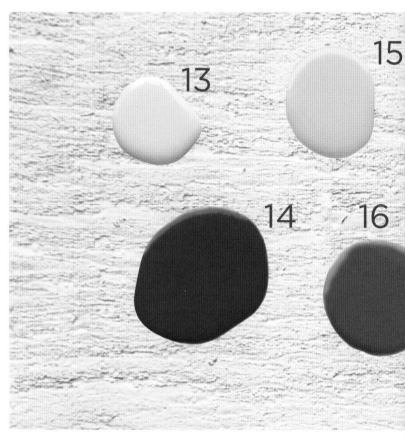

COOL COLORS

1. Benjamin Moore Berkshire Beige
2. Benjamin Moore Kendall Charcoal
3. Benjamin Moore Silver Satin
4. Benjamin Moore Celery Salt
5. Sherwin-Williams Modern Gray
6. Farrow & Ball Mouse's Back
7. Benjamin Moore Stormy Monday
8. Sherwin-Williams Manor House
9. Farrow & Ball Elephant's Breath
10. Farrow & Ball Blackened
11. Sherwin-Williams Quiver Tan
12. Farrow & Ball Clunch

WARM COLORS

13. Farrow & Ball Dimity
14. Sherwin-Williams Chateau Brown
15. Benjamin Moore Rich Cream
16. Benjamin Moore Maryville Brown
17. Sherwin-Williams Simplify Beige
18. Benjamin Moore Old Salem Gray
19. Benjamin Moore Burlap
20. Benjamin Moore Davenport Tan
21. Benjamin Moore Abingdon Putty
22. Farrow & Ball Cream
23. Benjamin Moore Winter Sky
24. Sherwin-Williams Medici Ivory

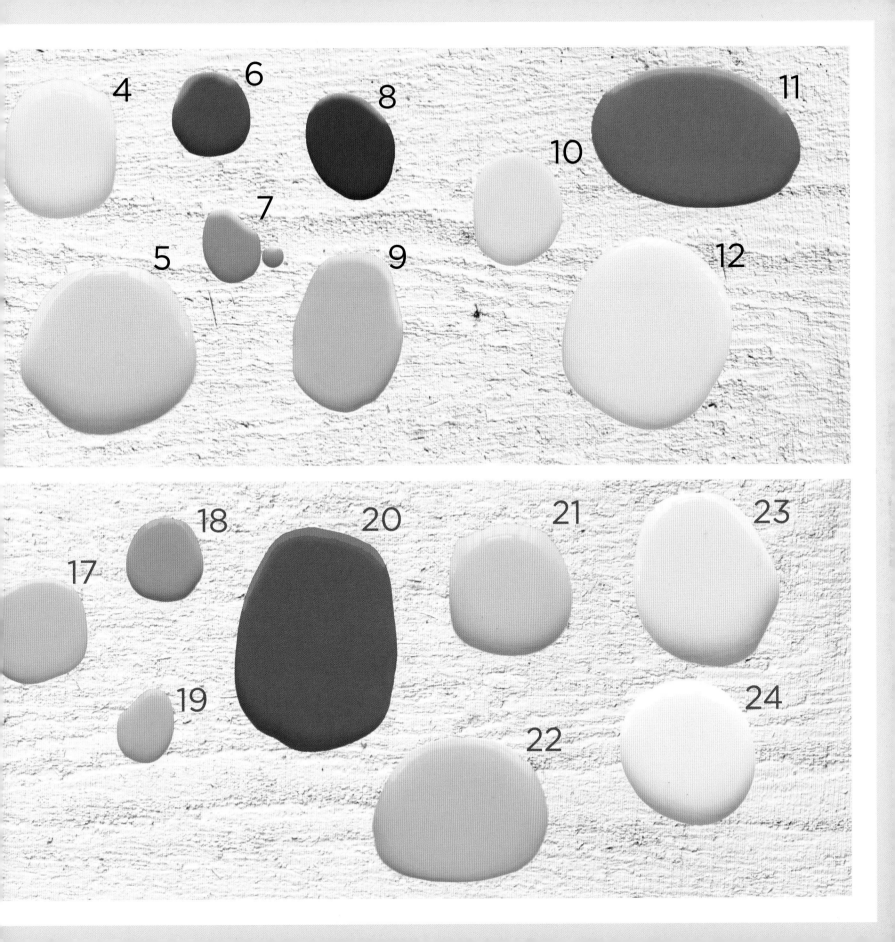

modern family

This clean and contemporary living room, as seen in the next spread, is the perfect introduction to the four key elements of a successful Nuanced Neutral interior. Shape abounds. The mix of straight and curved lines keeps the eye entertained. The shiny chrome of the table base, the nubby fabric on the armchair, the gloss of the coffee table, and the warm touches of wood throughout, comprise a broad diversity of textures. A wall of windows frames views of nature as if they were artwork.

From the bright white of the walls to the deepest black of the dining table, the room spans the entire spectrum of light to dark, creating a perfect backdrop for art and intentional pops of vivid color. The clean, open, gallery-like plan gives furniture, artwork, and personal objects their own space to shine, regardless of stylistic differences. What I find reassuring about this incredibly stylish living room is that it is home to a family of five and an appropriately colored, high-energy black Lab!

texture lecture

The following interior embodies the four core elements of Nuanced Neutral. The strong rectilinear components of the room—the framed artwork and coffee and end tables—are magnificently balanced by the sweeping arc of the sofa and the scribble-like presence of the leather butterfly chair.

Nature is represented in the stone of the floor, the touches of wood throughout, and the sculptural bromeliad plant on the Lucite table. In this interior the elements of texture and layer go hand in hand to create exceptional visual interest. The glass and polished aluminum of the lamp, the leather of the chair, the modern gridlike fabric of the sofa, the stone floor, and the great use of Lucite have all been deftly layered without any one texture taking center stage. The Lucite table is a brilliant addition because it works in the room without blocking the sight lines or visually cluttering up the space.

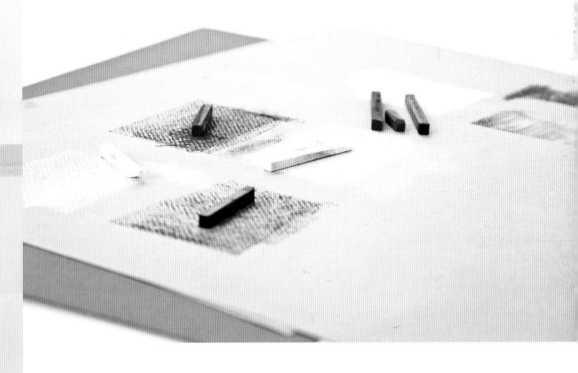

Subversive activities

Suburban homes

opposites attract

I love the sophistication and minimalism of this sleekly sexy bedroom. Even though the space looks straightforward, closer observation reveals a dynamic dialogue, a delicious flirtation between the key components in the space—soft versus hard, shiny versus matte, masculine versus feminine. An expanse of glass stands in stark contrast to the richly tactile shag rug. The straight lines of the bed bump up against the palpably female form of the undulating chaise.

The tension is heightened by the use of color and texture. The more masculine brown of the matte bedcover is tempered by the subtle sheen of shell pink velvet on the chaise. What should be noted here is that one great shape—in this case, the flea-market-find chaise—can make a room. The angularity of the artwork provides balance to the round tulip table, mirrored fireplace surround, and fluffy angora pillow on the bed.

balancing act

The happy commingling of multiple neutrals, both warm and cool, dark and light, makes the next space a genuinely inviting entryway. At first glance one sees a number of seemingly disparate elements—urban and country, modern and antique.

Through balance and symmetry of color, however, the various elements cohere. The linear aspects in the pottery, art, pillows, and architecture, for instance, bring these elements into harmony. The black pillow on the sofa echoes the black in the oil paintings. The warmth of the wooden chest bounces down to the rug and back up to the chestnut pillow panel.

The rug is a lesson in combining multiple neutral colors. There are so many different colors of yarn knotted into this rug, in subtle variations of shade—from pale gray to slate gray, from golden ivory to cocoa. Exploring how they interconnect to form a balanced palette is analogous to learning how to create a Nuanced Neutral interior.

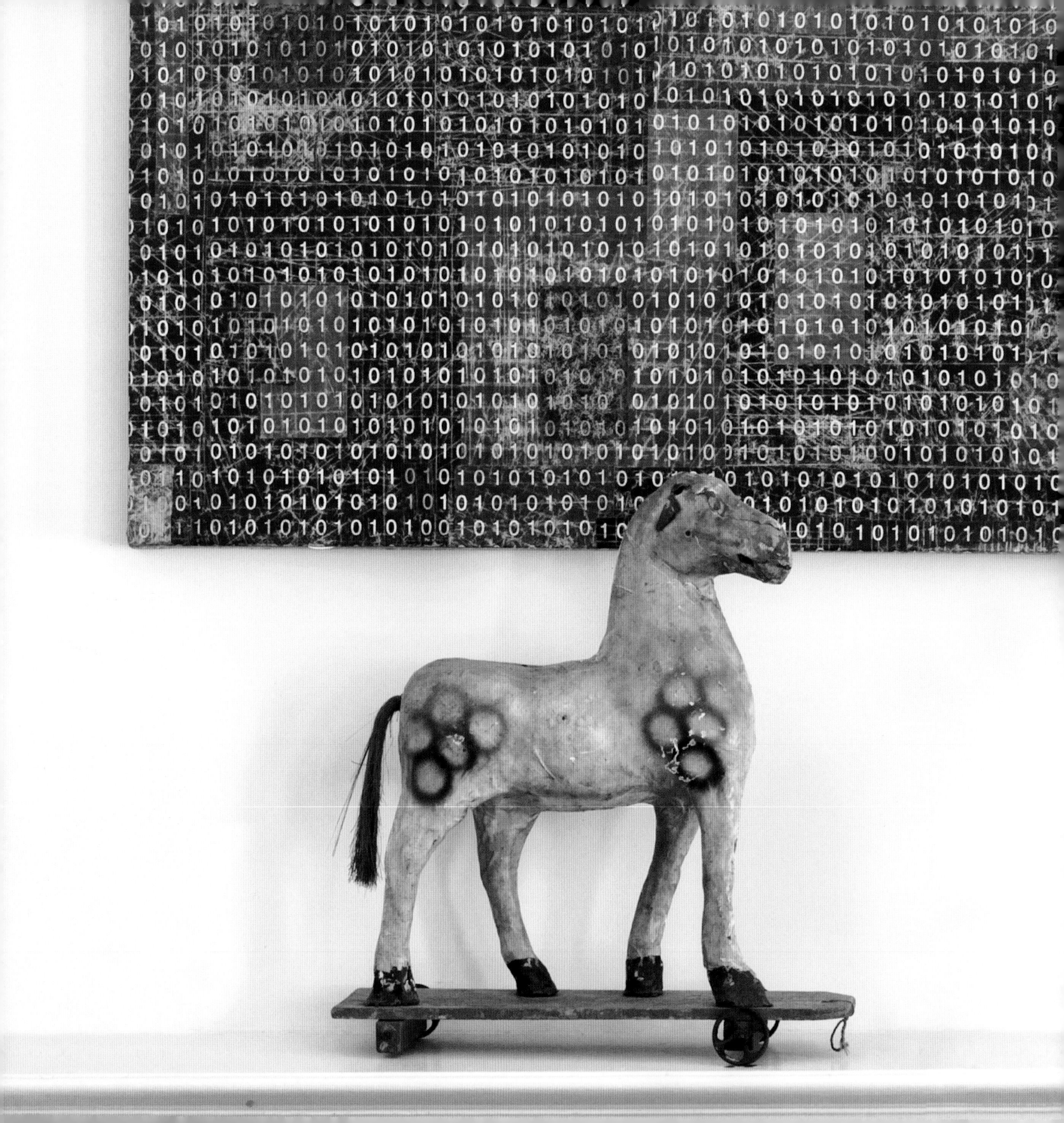

art-felt

The following living room is a veritable feast for the eyes. Despite how much artwork it contains, it feels comfortable and livable, never like a gallery, and it invites the viewer to relax and take in each intriguing object. Five different colors and textures of fabrics were used in this room, and the combination softens the scene.

All of the elements of Nuanced Neutral are represented here. Interesting shapes are everywhere, from the outline of the folk art horse and the sinewy vases on the mantel to the curve on the wing chair and the turned leg of the end table. Furniture shapes vary between rounded and straight-edge pieces. Textures that add depth and character to the room include the subtle but toothy upholstery fabric, the chunky weave to the rug, the smooth ceramic lamps, the patina of aged wood, and the layers of paint in the art. Nature appears in the five different wood finishes, the charming bowl of quail eggs, and the freshly picked ferns from Jane's garden. In the end it is the thoughtful layering of all these disparate bits that makes this space so appealing.

WARM CONTEMPORARY. The layers of linen, cotton twill, matelassé, and cotton, chosen in various neutral shades and set off by crisp white, make this bed inviting without being overwhelming. Keeping the bedding neatly tucked and foregoing the bed skirt enhances the modern look. If you were to add a skirt it should be tailored, not ruffled.

PALE PATTERN. Here is proof that white and ivory work beautifully together. Many people feel they need to commit to one, but I love a bed where the two play off each other. Collect linens in both white and ivory and have fun mixing them in different combinations. The simple addition of fresh white and ivory damask shams adds interest.

ROMANTIC WHITE. All the elements on this bed are white, but subtle differences in texture make each unique. Pin tucks, embroidery, varied sizes of ruffles, a vintage crocheted coverlet, and a pom-pom-fringed sham layer easily for an undeniably beautiful result.

GRAPHIC LUXURY. This bed has a hip, high-end-hotel aesthetic. In two different neutral shades, a bold graphic pattern works in conjunction with the pair of deep chocolate lines to add impact to the crisp white sheeting. The dark tailored bed skirt grounds the otherwise light bed.

nuanced neutral

Elegant in its simplicity, this outdoor dining area incorporates all the elements of Nuanced Neutral. Here the overarching element is nature, as represented by the stunningly verdant setting and underscored by the uncomplicated centerpiece of pots of herbs and the weathered wood of the benches. Straight and curved shapes balance one another. The smooth porcelain, in subtly different shades of white and cream, is layered happily with the shine of the silverware and the nubbiness of heavy linen napkins atop a smoother textured linen cloth. The whole setting is framed by matte painted architectural details. The final effect is one of ease and harmony.

cultured eclectic

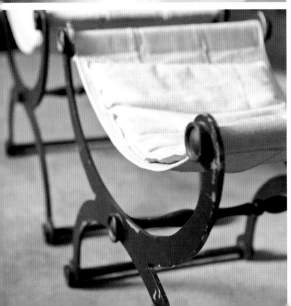

every room tells a story

This is a highly personal and educated style, created by gathering and displaying objects and art that resonate with and tell about the occupant. This revelatory quality is what makes an interior interesting not only to the inhabitant but to others as well. Seeing a Cultured Eclectic space is a bit like being a fly on the wall in someone's brain. Passions and peculiarities are owned up to; obsessions and oddities are embraced. Walls, surfaces, objects—everything in the room has something to say.

While every interior may be considered a reflection of its creator, Cultured Eclectic takes it further, reflecting the variety and depth of what interests the inhabitant. It is a style that develops over time as you combine your passions with panache.

When creating your own Cultured Eclectic space, ask yourself what backdrop would best suit your "installation" and what types of pieces you will include. Take the time to think about the objects you treasure and the result you seek. Do you want to conjure a nineteenth-century Italian country house, or are you channeling the Tate Modern? Once you have an initial vision, there are four key elements to consider layering into a Cultured Eclectic space:

UNEARTH CURIOSITIES. These are the quirky objects and oddities, often from nature, that call to you because they are purely interesting. They usually make great conversation pieces as people ponder what the objects are and how and why you acquired them. Fossils, petrified wood, and insects are just a few examples of the myriad pieces that can play a role in your eclectic puzzle.

SHARE YOUR PERSONALITY. While all the elements of Cultured Eclectic are imbued with personality, these objects have a one-of-a-kind feel to them; whether they are hand-stitched, carved, or figurative in form, they somehow evoke human emotion and add warmth and humor to a space.

CURATE YOUR COLLECTIONS. Whether or not you can explain your attraction to certain objects, the things you are drawn to and those you save are an expression of you. Any collections you have should be thoughtfully displayed; this will help give them coherence and presence.

EMBRACE ART. Surround yourself with pieces you love for reasons beyond their simple decorative appeal. Include a mix of fine art, your children's art, and found objects, and display them in a creative manner. Remember, art is in the eye of the beholder!

Three of the finished rooms in this section are the very personal expression of the artist Frank Faulkner. He is southern, a gentleman, an intellectual, and a wonderful storyteller—and his house reflects each of these traits. When it comes to form, proportion, and color, Faulkner has an artistic sensibility, and because he is confident in his tastes he is also comfortable mixing high and low. In short, he is a master of the Cultured Eclectic aesthetic, and there is much to learn from the way in which each of his rooms becomes an extended exploration of his many interests.

cultured eclectic
fabrics

I started collecting fabrics at the age of six and never looked back. Fortunately, I have created a job for myself that makes indulging this passion tax deductible! On these two spreads are textiles from my collection that I consider Cultured Eclectic.

I advocate using neutral solids in leather, linen, velvet, or wool for larger upholstered pieces, then layering in eclectic fabrics, such as the ones pictured here, as accents. Each tells a story of the culture from which it came. I am always seeking to add techniques to my collection and I collect all shapes and sizes of textiles, from small scraps of embroidery to Afghani tent dividers.

You can pick up pieces that appeal to you as you travel, or at thrift shops, flea markets, and antique stores. Try using an interesting textile cut to fit a worn tabletop, and cover it with glass for a special customized look. There is really no piece too small, as almost anything can be framed as art or stitched up into a unique pillow or valance.

1. Indonesian batik

2. Shibori or tie-dye

3. Japanese: resist (protective coating) on cotton crêpe

4. Javanese: wax resist, multicolored technique

5. Indian: indigo resist

6. Chinese: lovely silk-on-silk embroidery

7. African: mud cloth or bogolanfini

8. Balinese: resist technique

9. Chinese resist

10. Peruvian patchwork

11. Embroidered trim

12. Afghani Suzani embroidery

13. Kashmiri crewelwork

14. South American Mola work

15. Crewelwork

15

curiosities

Cabinets of curiosities, *Wunderkammer* (German for "wonder room"), date back to the 1500s, when collectors attempted to catalogue the world around them. The rooms were indeed wonderful to behold, filled with peculiar creatures, insects, and shells, their arrangement usually as interesting as the specimens themselves. These curiosities were often the founding collections of now-famous natural history museums.

The Enlightenment Gallery at the British Museum and the Soane Museum, both located in London, are wonderful places to get inspiration and a better understanding of this element. Their collections are also beautifully displayed, offering many ideas and inspirations for showcasing your own curiosities.

Fast-forward to today and think of adding items to your collection of objects that are not only visually stimulating or appealing but that push you online to seek more information. This is about unusual (not necessarily beautiful) and thought-provoking objects. For instance, the early Victorian horn chair pictured (near right) is a quirky favorite of mine (it lives in my office). It is not pretty, but it most certainly had a story to tell when I ran across it in an antique shop and couldn't leave without it. Not everyone loves it, but they always ask about it!

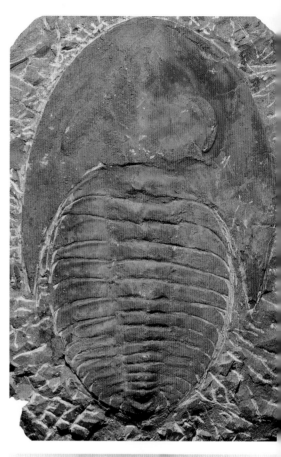

personality

Objects, like people, exude personality. This element comprises everyday objects—perhaps found at tag sales or antique stores—that have something special to say to the world. Through their aged look, handmade feel, or delicate craftsmanship, they often have a one-of-a-kind quality. They are quirky and fun, and they make you smile.

The polar bear lamp is one of my favorite possessions. I saw him across a crowded flea market field and it was love at first sight! Something in his expression not only spoke but yelled to me, "Take me home!" Though I hoped he wasn't too expensive, I knew I would buy him even if he was. I still can't explain what it is about the lamp that brings me joy, I just know it does.

The unbelievably detailed crazy quilt was crafted using the scraps from peoples' lives. Each patch has something to say and is visually enchanting at the same time. It is filled with stories that I can only speculate about, but that is half the fun of the piece.

The hide-covered trunk was a gift from my grandmother when I was little and it has followed me throughout my life. It commands attention in every space it inhabits.

The ivory frogs belong to Frank Faulkner and the fun found-object metal dog sculpture belongs to a dear friend and colleague.

collections

My grandmother started my first collection of antique dolls, and my mother helped me add to it year after year. My mother collected quilts, Shaker furniture, and bird engravings, so we were constantly on the prowl at flea markets, yard sales, antique auctions, and stores.

I've always taken a lighthearted, hunt-and-gather approach to collecting rather than an academic one. I'm drawn to pretty things such as light blue and white Staffordshire plates (page 209), unusually decorative things such as stick-and-ball furniture (opposite), and quirky, funny things such as my conch shell tourist art. (On its own it can look tacky, but massed and mounted, it goes from clutter to culture.) It's an urge, a calling, a sort of addiction—one that can quickly become a storage nightmare if you collect beyond what you have room to display.

The beauty—as explained in one of my favorite books, *In Flagrante Collecto*—is that you can collect anything. Once united with others of their kind, seemingly random objects are elevated to more than the sum of their parts.

To give your passion the impact and power it deserves, research ways to display what you have. Many things can be hung on walls, but others defy gravity and need to be shelved. Some objects look best under glass, while others can be pushpinned into any surface. Start with a simple Web search for "displaying collections," which will bring up myriad creative solutions and inspirations.

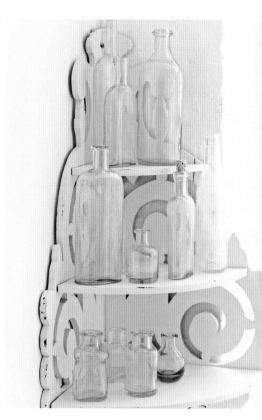

collections

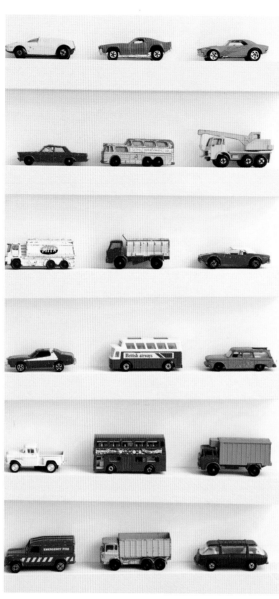

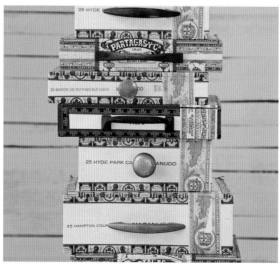

GVSTAV
KLIMT
NACHLASS

art

Art is an intuitive rather than rational form of self-expression in which the meanings are malleable. Its appeal, importance, and message are an unspoken, deeply personal conversation between you and the artwork. It's through exposure to various forms of art that you will discover what appeals to you. Everything you see educates your eye about color, scale, proportion, and technique, preparing you to find pieces on your own. You may not always love a work of art, but it may stir an emotional response within you, and often it shifts your beliefs or understanding in some slight or profound way—forcing you to look at the world differently.

I advocate surrounding yourself with art that moves you in a positive way. Curate your own collection of pieces that speak to you. Make it personal and stay open to new and emerging forms of expression. Don't fear mixing different mediums in one space; photography, sculpture, painting, and drawing happily coexist. It is the interesting juxtaposition of different eras and styles as well as mediums of art that make a Cultured Eclectic space work. Children's art can hang happily beside fine art, and found objects displayed as art can live in the same space with modern sculpture and primitive art. Things you love will always find a way to be at home with one another.

accessible art

Each of the installations on this spread is more about creativity than cash. This is a small sampling of ideas for creating art through creative display.

1. METAL TOOLS. This arrangement of everyday metal objects from bygone eras is graphic, graceful, and makes a huge impact on a stark white wall. The artful interplay between the unique outlines and the "What did they use that for?" questions the objects elicit makes the arrangement interesting.

2. WRITING PAPER CLIPPED AND COLLAGED. This piece consists simply of snippets of letterheads from old writing paper glued to a piece of acid-free paper and framed.

3. REPURPOSING FOUND OBJECTS. These old wreath forms have been resurrected as a display on a richly colored blank wall.

4. DISPLAYING PHOTOS, ETC. This fun, fluid, and functional format is as easy as mounting two metal bars (cost: about four dollars) on a wall, a door—anywhere you have the space—at a distance that allows you to display photos, postcards, or doodles. The best part is that you can move the images around at will.

5. FABRIC SCRAPS ON EMBROIDERY HOOPS. I saw this idea online and was blown away by what an easy and inexpensive way this is to display fabrics (wrapping paper and wallpaper work, too). The fact that it is a series of circles makes the grouping particularly appealing.

6. NEWSPAPER AND SHOPPING BAG ART. These two prints hang in Frank Faulkner's bathroom. The rhino was cut from an early Banana Republic shopping bag and the ostrich skeleton was cut from the *The New York Times*. The old, beat-up frames add character and lend an antiquarian flair.

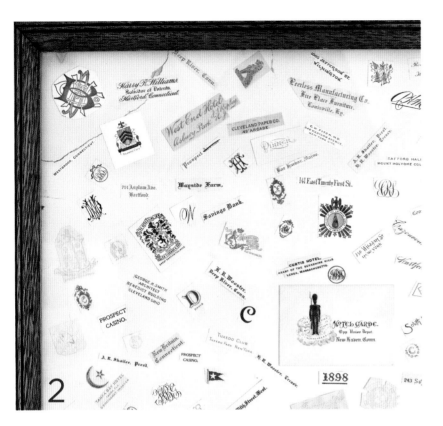

mise-en-scène

Frank Faulkner's vision for his salon and adjoining dining room was to re-create the feeling of a timeworn, slightly dilapidated nineteenth-century Italian country house that happened to come with all the modern conveniences. There is a brilliant theatricality to the spaces, but it is subtle, so they remain elegant, inviting, and livable. Faulkner has expertly fused neoclassical and African motifs, and the sprinkling of thought-provoking found objects—ranging in scale from tiny to huge, and in value from precious to pedestrian—epitomizes the Cultured Eclectic aesthetic.

Every surface and object in this Hudson, New York, home has a story to tell. The oversized bust, on the following page, started out in Franco Zeffirelli's production of *Antony and Cleopatra*. The round marble tables flanking the sofa came from the Art Deco cruise ship the S.S. *Europa*. The Mende mask atop the stack of books (next spread, center) was worn in ritual coming-of-age dances by members of the oldest secret society of women on record. The list goes on, and it's fascinating.

As is often a hallmark in the best of Cultured Eclectic interiors, high and low live harmoniously side by side. The curtains, made from lengths of the humblest unbleached muslin, are fastened with plastic shower curtain rings intended to mimic real ivory. The sheers, added to filter the light, were purchased at Wal-Mart for practically nothing.

mise en scène (continued)

In Frank's adjoining dining room, the windows, walls, and floors are treated in the same manner as those in the salon. The plaster walls were stripped of their paper and left without any further treatment—their irregularities add a depth and patina to the space that can only come from age.

The floors in both the salon and the dining room are painted a stone color that is nearly as light as the walls, blurring the usual horizon line that occurs when darker floors meet lighter walls. This trick allows everything in the composition to show up; nothing is lost. Threadbare Oriental rugs are thoughtfully framed by the sea grass beneath, making the transition to the floor less visually abrupt. Frank's masterfully layered painting completes the Cultured Eclectic scene, beautifully encompassing the elements of art and personality.

PHILIP ZIEGLER

TOM REISS

HARDSON

ROY STRONG CREATING SMALL GARDENS

Suzy Menkes THE WINDSOR Style

Carolyne Roehm PRESENTATIONS

Jean Cocteau

Maurizio Fagiolo dell'Arco Great Baroque and Rococo Sculpture

SAFARI

ARSHILE GORKY RAND

Country Living COUNTRY GARDENS

DREAM HOUSES

20th Century

The Pritzker ARCHITECTURE PRIZE THE FIRST TWENT

BRIDGES THROUGH MY EYES

DAVID HOCKNEY BY

AT HOME IN SCO

THE ENGLISH COUNTRY HOME Edited by V

HOMETOWN USA

CUVIER'S ANIMALS: 3b1 Illustrations from the Classic Nineteenth-Cen

THE DECORATOR Florence de Dampierre

Harter ANIMALS: 1419 Copyright-Free Illustrations Dover 0-486-23766-5

HOME DECORATOR'S BIBLE PERIOD FIREPLACES

letter of the law

Built as a law office in the mid-1880s, Frank Faulkner's house is in and of itself an object of desire. The inherent beauty of its proportions and scale, its soaring twelve-foot ceilings, exceptional windows, lovely chestnut paneling, and marbleized slate fireplaces create a rich backdrop for this example of the Cultured Eclectic style. The bookcases that formerly housed a law library have been repurposed for Frank's library on art and design. I happily envision spending a perfect weekend in the guest room on the next spread, just getting lost in the pages of all the fabulous books.

The far wall is anchored by the stately slate fireplace and Frank's painting above it, entitled *Helios*. Four works flanking them, including the sepia bust print (a flea market find from Bath, England), help balance the strength of the wall of books. The russet hues of the exquisite Victorian paisley bedcover are picked up in the throw on the comfy overstuffed armchair and again in the sepia print. A broad assortment of styles and periods of furniture, art, and objects keeps the eye entertained. The neutral treatment of the floor adds a restful sense of restraint to the otherwise richly appointed room.

natural selection

The stylish dining room that follows gets its energy from a fusion of rough industrial architecture and refined old-world naturalist ingredients. Ink stamps on the brick wall hint at the space's former life as a shipping warehouse. In considering whether to paint over these vestiges, I decided the walls were a curiosity with an authentic story to tell, so they were scrubbed clean and left alone. From afar, the repetitive color and pattern they create reminded me of birch bark. This realization inspired me to adopt the organic, woodland scheme reflected in the collection of egg prints, the leafy chandelier, the wooden mushroom centerpiece, and the regal pheasant that presides over the scene.

The space once felt cavernous, unwelcoming. Now the industrial metal and reclaimed wood table anchors and defines the space, and the curvaceous, overscale wing chairs soften it. A showstopping, personality-packed palm frond chandelier, salvaged from a grand hotel ballroom, was purposely hung close to the table to lend a more intimate focus to the room.

I adopted the color palette from the multiple shades of green in the meandering leaves of the crewel curtains and introduced the colors throughout the room in various ways, from the speckles of the eggs in the collection of prints to the mounded moss and the rich color of the painted wall. The green scheme gets pops of drama from the red faux bois side table and from the small but sensual touches of classic leopard.

HOW-TO: hanging a collection

1. Start with a collection of framed art.

2. Using craft paper, trace and cut out the outline of each frame.

3. Mark the spot where the center top of the frame's hanging wire hits the paper.

4. Place the traced paper cutouts on the wall to mock up the grouping.

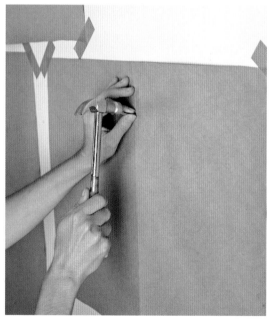

5. Hammer the placement nail through the paper at the spot where you marked the top of the hanging wire and remove the paper from the wall.

6. Hang the art and enjoy!

FLIRTING WITH
cultured eclectic

My mother and I fell in love with these prints in Uppsala, Sweden, on an architectural tour. The intricacy and delicate gradations of color in the feathers and the interplay between the varied shapes of the birds led us to hang them as a collection. Sticking to a single style of frame keeps one's eyes on the beautiful birds.

I consider the antique chest below to be a curiosity, due to the smoke painting technique, also known as fumage, used to decorate it. The smoky effect is achieved by capturing the ephemeral quality of candle smoke. It is a rare and unique piece that demands further inspection. Finally, the cockatoo statuette adds a dash of aristocratic personality.

HOW-TO: dressing the cultured eclectic bed

ANTIQUE CHIC. Vintage quilts are truly works of art, so beautifully made that many are still useable today. Freshen up the look by adding a solid linen skirt, duvet, and shams in a complementary color. The crochet-edge sheeting keeps the antique look alive. For a modern look, try a geometric patchwork quilt on a platform bed.

RAJASTHANI REVERIE. Always drawn to exquisitely detailed ethnic textiles, I like to balance them with swaths of solid, coordinating colors to give the eye a rest. The intricately quilted satin coverlet in rich persimmon and the velvet pillow work well together because both colors appear in the amazing mirrorwork spread and shams.

HIGH-END HIPPIE. Personality and pattern strike a pose on this bed. A Kantha-stitched Indian bedcover, a vintage Victorian piano shawl, and pillow crafted from a 1960s scarf seem like unlikely bedfellows, but the green, turquoise, pink, and red all appear at least two times on the bed. The pattern is broken up by the use of coordinating solids.

SUNRISE, SUNSET. Another gorgeous, hand-stitched bedcover takes center stage, guiding the palette for this sophisticated bed. This Indian coverlet is feminine but it stays unfussy and feels refined. The restful sea glass blue/green is picked up in the sheeting and solid linen accessories. The multiple hues of pink are echoed in the hand-knit throw.

I am grateful for so much and so many. Getting to this point has been a wonderful journey because I have had the friendship and support of amazing people every step along the way.

First and foremost thanks to my unwaveringly creative, supportive, endlessly flexible, perennially upbeat, and

contributions. Without each of you I would never have been able to do what I do!

Thanks to: Jill Cohen, my tireless agent, whose vision made this book a possibility • Doris Cooper and everyone at Clarkson Potter for seeing its potential and letting us "go with it" • Aliza Fogelson for her

acknowledgments

wildly talented team, without whom this book would not and could not have come to fruition.

And to the entire staff of the Annie Selke Companies, whose dedication, enthusiasm and continued support kept everything moving in the right direction and have made it possible for me to realize my dreams. You are my extended family. I honor your individual gifts and

dogged commitment to getting it right, getting it done, and always making it better • Kindra Clineff, our location photographer, who "got it" from the get-go and was always a pleasure • Googie for letting us beg,

borrow, and steal from her world on almost a daily basis • Will Laidlaw for always, always being there to lend a hand or make me laugh •

Kelley for the power hugs that keep me going • Lucy and Charlie, whose generosity, support, and love mean the world to me • WWT for keeping the wine flowing and the trips delightful • Nancy K. for explaining some of the finer points of life • Patti, Stephen, Frank, Joan, and John for being as passionately voyeuristic as I am and for the help and advice doled out in many a motor coach across the

Atlantic • Jane Kasten, whose approach to home is nothing short of inspired • Jaime Kelly for her tireless editing, her gentle prodding, and her adorable house • Frank Faulkner and Philip Kensinger for their uniquely personal approach to art and to the art of living • FT Architects for their flair for and commitment to contem-

porary architecture and design • Steve for providing balance and the critically important escape key • Jess for keeping me moving in the right direction and in the right place at the right time • my friends at Vanguard Furniture and P. Kaufmann, who continue to help me complete the thought • Jon Smith Jr. and Ed Gottesman

for giving me a master class in business one day at a time • Roger Goldman for being such a wise and wonderful

fan • Jan Williams for her insight and her commitment to making everything better and clearer. You have taught me so much about myself and those around me. • Marie, who has a gift with cut and color • The Bod Squad: JD for getting it tight and Christine for keeping it loose • Boo Powell, Hillary Lambert, and Jamie Coffey, who have always kept

business fun, friendly, and forward-looking.

resources

There are so many fabulous home design resources out there. These shops and companies are some of my favorite sources for products and inspiration.

NATIONAL

The Annie Selke Companies
annieselke.com
dashandalbert.com
freshamerican.com
pineconehill.com

Calico Corners
calicocorners.com

Cottage & Bungalow
cottageandbungalow.com

Electrolux
electrolux.com

Frank Faulkner (artist)
frankfaulkner.com

FT Architecture
Peter Franck and Kathleen Triem
518-392-3721
ftarchitecture.com

Garnet Hill
garnethill.com

Adam Gudeon (artist)
adamgudeon.com

Jo-Ann Fabric & Craft
joann.com
Annie Selke Home Fabrics

KraftMaid (kitchen design and cabinetry)
kraftmaid.com

Lavender Fields
415 E. Main Street
Port Jefferson, NY 11777
866-898-5461
lavenderfieldsonline.com

Layla Grayce
laylagrayce.com

Melissa Matsuki Lillie (artist)
melissalillie.com

Neiman Marcus
neimanmarcus.com

Nemo Tile
nemotile.com

Porter & Plunk (antiques)
porterandplunk.com

Posh Tots
poshtots.com

Silestone
silestone.com

Sundance
sundancecatalog.com

Surface View (murals)
surfaceview.com

Vanguard Furniture
vanguardfurniture.com

NORTHEAST

Connecticut

Comina
comina.com
Nine locations throughout Connecticut, Massachusetts, and Rhode Island

Design Solutions
146 Elm St.
New Canaan, CT 06840
866-903-3744
designsolutionstore.com

Katahdin Furniture
60 Whitney Ave.
New Haven, CT 06510
203-777-5551

Lillian August
32 Knight St.
Norwalk, CT 06851
203-847-1596
lillianaugust.com

Lynnens, Inc.
278 Greenwich Ave.
Greenwich, CT 06830
203-629-3659
lynnens.com

Palooza
1636 Post Rd.
Fairfield, CT 06824
203-255-3655

Delaware

Bayside Rug Company
35131 Lighthouse Rd.
Selbyville, DE 19975
302-436-5652
baysiderugco.com

Simply Home
3628 Concord Pike
Wilmington, DE 19803
302-477-0999
visitsimplyhome.com

Maine

The Cherished Home
31 Searsport Ave.
Belfast, ME 04915
207-338-4111
thecherishedhome.com

Margo Moore Interiors
74 Elm St.
Camden, ME 04843
207-236-4596
margomoore.com

Massachusetts

Best of the Beach
2 Straight Wharf
Nantucket, MA 02554
508-228-6263
bestofthebeachnantucket.com

Hudson
312 Shawmut Ave.
Boston, MA 02118
617-292-0090
hudsonboston.com

Margo's Practically Unusual
27 Wianno Ave.
Osterville, MA 02655
508-428-5664
margoshome.com

O'Rama's
148 Washington St.
Marblehead, MA 01945
781-631-0894

Osgood's
333 Park St.
West Springfield, MA 01089
888-674-6638
osgoodtextile.com

RPM Carpets & Floor Coverings
192 Rte. 137
East Harwich, MA 02645
508-432-4151
rpmcarpets.com

The Rug Merchant LLC
11 B Commerce Rd.
Rockland, MA 02370
781-331-5505
therugmerchant.com

The Welch Company
132 Front St.
Scituate, MA 02066
781-545-1400
welchcompany.com

White Magdelena House
60 South St.
Hingham, MA 02043
781-749-0048

Wishbasket
50 Water St.
Newburyport, MA 01950
978-465-1515

Maryland
Ani Kasten Ceramics
Baltimore, MD
anipots.com

The House Downtown
524 E. Belvedere Sq.
Baltimore, MD 21212
410-464-1440
thehousedowntown.com

Shoemaker Country
8095 Main St.
Ellicott City, MD 21043
410-461-5552
shoemakercountry.net

Urban Country
7117 Arlington Rd.
Bethesda, MD 20814
301-654-0500
urbancountrydesign.com

New Hampshire
Nashua Wallpaper Co.
129 W. Pearl St.
Manchester, NH 03060
603-882-9491
universaldecor.com

Ruggles & Hunt
8 Westminister St.
Walpole, NH 03608
603-756-9607

New Jersey
Ashton-Whyte Bed & Bath
250 S. Main St.
Pennington, NJ 08534
609-737-7171
ashtonwhyte.com

Between the Sheets
1012 Central Ave.
Ship Bottom, NJ 08008
609-361-9297

Philosophy
58 Main St.
Chester, NJ 07930
908-879-0055
philosophyboutique.com

Saplings
242 Bloomfield Ave.
Caldwell, NJ 07006
973-228-3300
saplingsusa.com

Semplice
465 Bloomfield Ave.
Montclair, NJ 07042
973-783-7495
semplicehome.com

Shelter Home
704 Cookman Ave.
Asbury Park, NJ 07712
732-774-7790
shelterhome.com

Sickles Market
1 Harrison Ave.
Little Silver, NJ 07739
732-741-9563
sicklesmarket.com

Stella e Luna
500 Bay Ave.
Pt. Pleasant Beach, NJ 08742
732-714-2221

Trouvaille
12 Beechwood Rd.
Summit, NJ 07901
908-273-1400
trouvaillesummit.com

Wostbrock Home
225 Goffle Rd.
Ridgewood, NJ 07450
201-445-0807
wostbrockhome.com

New York
A&G Merch
111 N. 6th St.
Brooklyn, NY 11211
718-388-1779
aandgmerch.com

Ashbourne Designs
380 New York Ave.
Huntington, NY 11743
631-547-5252
ashbournedesigns.com

Down & Quilt Shop
518 Columbus Ave.
New York, NY 10024
212-496-8980
downquiltshop.com

East India Designs
101 Pondfield Rd.
Bronxville, NY 10708
914-337-2177
eastindiadesigns.com

Environment 337
337 Smith St.
Brooklyn, NY 11231
718-522-1767
environment337.com

Fishers
144 Main St.
Sag Harbor, NY 11963
631-725-0006
fishershomefurnishings.com

Gracious Home
212-517-6300
gracioushome.com
Two locations in New
York City

Hammertown Barn
3201 Rte. 199
Pine Plains, NY 12567
518-398-7075
hammertownbarn.com

Hammertown Barn
6420 Montgomery Street
Rhinebeck, NY 12572
845-876-1450
hammertownbarn.com

High Falls Mercantile
113 Main St.
High Falls, NY 12440
800-687-6707
highfallsmercantile.com

Hildreth's
51-55 Main St.
Southampton, NY 11968
631-283-2300
hildreths.com

Next Summer
4955 Lake Shore Dr.
Bolton Landing, NY 12814
518-644-2774

Painting With Flowers
298 Main St.
Port Washington, NY 11050
516-883-4164
paintingwithflowersltd.com

Sue Leal (decorative
painting)
10 Whitings Pond Rd.
Canaan, NY
dewdropart.com

Wendy Gee
1949 Palmer Ave.
Larchmont, NY 10538
914-834-8507
wendygee.com

Pennsylvania
Ashton-Whyte Bed & Bath
835 Lancaster Ave.
Bryn Mawr, PA 19010
610-525-7556

UpHome
138 E. King St.
Malvern, PA 19355
484-318-7109
uphomeltd.com

Upriver Home
202 Broad St.
Milford, PA 18337
570-296-2026
upriverhome.com

Rhode Island
The Cottage at Four
Corners
3847 Main Rd.
Tiverton, RI 02878
401-625-5814
thecottageri.com

Dove & Distaff Rug Gallery
365 Main St.
Wakefield, RI 02879
401-284-1170
doveanddistaffruggallery.com

Vermont
Clementine
58 Main St.
Middlebury, VT 05753
802-388-4442
clementinestore.com

Dragonfly Dry Goods
136 Main St.
Brattleboro, VT 05301
802-257-0099
dragonflydrygoods.com

Stowe Kitchen, Bath &
Linen
1813 Mountain Rd.
Stowe, VT 05672
802-253-8050
stowekitchen.net

SOUTHEAST
Alabama
Alabama Furniture Market
10 Commercial Park Dr.
Calera, AL 35040
205-668-9995
alabamafuruniture
emarket.com

Harmony Landing
2925 18th St. South
Homewood, AL 35209
205-871-0585
harmonylanding.com

The Ivy Cottage
2401 Old Shell Rd.
Mobile, AL 36607
251-473-4438
theivycottageonline.com

The Linen Closet
1653 North McFarland Blvd.
no. G2F
Tuscaloosa, AL 35406
877-376-8951
thelinenclosetonline.com

Marguerite's Conceits
2406 Canterbury Rd.
Birmingham, AL 35223
205-879-2730

Objects
30500 State Hwy. 181,
no. 310
Spanish Fort, AL 36527
251-626-7225

Three Sheets
2904 18th St. S.
Birmingham, AL 35209
205-871-2337

Arkansas
Cobblestone & Vine
5100 Kavanaugh Blvd.
Little Rock, AR 72207
501-664-4249
cobblestoneandvine.com

House to Home
4328 Central Ave.
Hot Springs, AR 71913
501-520-4949
shophousetohome.com

M. Grace
3511 SE J Street, no. 4
Bentonville, AR 72712
866-524-7049
mgracenet.com

Florida
Duh
501 N. Ninth Ave.
Pensacola, FL 32501
850-439-0640
duhpensacola.com

The Green Door
32 Ave. D
Apalachicola, FL 32320
850-653-1424
amysgreendoor.com

Jaffe Oriental Rug Gallery
8206 Philips Hwy., no. 18
Jacksonville, FL 32256
904-730-2121
jafferuggallery.com

Joseph's Cottage
319 Reid Ave.
Port St. Joe, FL 32456
850-227-7877
josephscottage.com

Kreativa for Kids
13482 SW 131st St.
Miami, FL 33186
305-251-1955
kreativaforkids.com

Kreativa for Kids
1430 S. Dixie Hwy.
Coral Gables, FL 33146
305-284-0525
kreativaforkids.com

Loggia Home & Garden
1882 Old Dixie Hwy.
Vero Beach, FL 32960
772-770-3009
loggiahomeandgarden.com

Main Street Traders
1468 Main St.
Sarasota, FL 34236
941-373-0475
mainstreettraders.com

Seaside Chic
217 W. Venice Ave.
Venice, FL 34285
941-483-1177
shopseasidechic.com

Snappy Turtle
1100 E. Atlantic Ave.
Delray Beach, FL 33483
561-276-8088
snappy-turtle.com

Style Key West
313 Margaret St.
Key West, FL 33040
305-292-4004
stylekeywest.com

Georgia
Erika Reade
3732 Roswell Rd.
Atlanta, GA 30342
404-233-3857
erikareade.com

Gatewood Hall
165 Depot St.
Blue Ridge, GA 30513
706-946-6246

Heery's TOO
184 E. Clayton St.
Athens, GA 30601
706-552-3886
Heerys.com

Isabel's
3121 Vineville Ave
Macon, GA 31204
478-744-0909
isabelslinens.com

Mish Mash
536 Grand Slam Dr.
Evans, GA 30809
706-814-7380

One Fish Two Fish
401 Whitaker St.
Savannah, GA 31401
912-447-4600
onefishstore.com

Terra Cottage
1183 Howell Mill Rd. NW
Atlanta, GA 30318
404-350-0330
terracottagellc.com

The Tree House
112 N. Main St.
Clayton, GA 30552
706-782-7297

Kentucky
Mercantile
2000 Frankfort Ave.
Louisville, KY 40206
502-899-1699

Mulberry & Lime
216 N. Limestone St.
Lexington, KY 40507
859-231-0800
mulberryandlime.com

Simple Changes
561 N. Lake Dr.
Prestonsburg, KY 41653
606-886-7040
simplechanges.net

Louisiana
The Chartreuse Pear
108 N. Vienna St.
Ruston, LA 71270
308-255-7327

Hestia Linens
61D Park Place Dr.
Covington, LA 70433
985-893-0490
hestialinens.com

Mississippi
Franklin Cruise
515 Cruise St.
Corinth, MS 38834
662-287-8069
franklincruise.com

North Carolina
About Last Night
377 U.S. Hwy. 70 S.
Hickory, NC 28602
828-324-2830

Coastal Accents
107 Ark Ct.
Poplar Branch, NC 27965
252-453-3501

Cottage Chic
100 W. Main St.
Aberdeen, NC 28315
910-944-0501
cottagechicstore.com

Cottage Chic
1232 E. Blvd.
Charlotte, NC 28203
704-375-1888
cottagechicstore.com

Dolce Dimora
803D Friendly Center Rd.
Greensboro, NC 27408
336-282-9572
dolcedimora.com

Dovecote
2000 Fearrington Village
Pittsboro, NC 27312
919-542-1145
fearrington.com/village/
dovecote.asp

GDC Home
695 Coleman Blvd.
Mt. Pleasant, NC 29464
843-849-0711
gdchome.com

GDC Home
420 Fresh Fields Drive
John's Island, NC 29455
843-768-4246
gdchome.com

Homestead Fine Linens
110 N. Main St.
Hendersonville, NC 28792
828-697-8787

Lavender & Lace
2031 Cameron St.
Raleigh, NC 27605
919-828-6007
lavenderandlace.net

Meg Brown Home
Furnishings
5491 U.S. Hwy. 158
Advance, NC 27006
336-998-7277
megbrownhome.com

The Painted Cottage
6692 Beach Dr.
Ocean Isle, NC 28469
910-579-5995

Porter & Prince
6 Brook St.
Asheville, NC 28803
828-277-2337
porterandprince.com

This Little Cottage
41934 NC Highway 12
Avon, NC 27915
252-995-3320
thislittlecottage.com

The Very Thing
2100 S. Church St.
Burlington, NC 27215
336-226-6066

South Carolina
Coastal Chic
41 Plantation Park Dr., no.
300
Bluffton, SC 29910
843-815-6611
coastalchic.com

Cottage & Vine
4600 Forest Dr.
Columbia, SC 29206
803-787-7985

Currents
10185 Ocean Hwy.
Pawleys Island, SC 29585
843-235-0456

Finishing Touches Etc.
917 Bay St.
Beaufort, SC 29902
843-522-1716

Glendinning Home
Collection
78G Arrow Road
Hilton Head, SC 29928
843-785-4272
ghconline.com

GDC Home
1290 Sam Rittenberg Blvd.
Charleston, SC 29407
843-571-1027
gdchome.com

Tennessee
Bella Vita
3670 Houston Levee Rd.
Collierville, TN 38017
901-850-0892
shopbellavita.com

The Furniture Shoppe
1903 E. 24th St. Place
Chattanooga, TN 37404
423-493-7630
thefurnitureshoppe.net

Gild the Lily
5101 Sanderlin Ave.
Memphis, TN 38117
901-682-8277

O.P. Jenkins
209 W. Summit Hill Dr.
Knoxville, TN 37902
865-522-9632
opjenkinsfurniture.com

Peddler Gift Shop
1756 West Northfield Blvd.
Murfreesboro, TN 37129
615-896-5431
peddlerinteriors.com

Pembroke Antiques
6610 Hwy. 100
Nashville, TN 37205
615-353-0889

Rebecca's Furniture and
Design
341 Main St.
Franklin, TN 37064
615-595-2553
rebeccasfurniture.com

Virginia

Chesapeake & Crescent
Home
24 N. Main St.
Kilmarnock, VA 22482
804-435-8800
chesapeakecrescent.com

The Globe
221 Laskin Rd.
Virginia Beach, VA 23451
757-422-3313
theglobevirginia
beach.com

Patina Antiques
2171 Ivy Rd.
Charlottesville, VA 22903
434-244-3222

The Red Barn Mercantile
113 S. Columbus St.
Alexandria, VA 22314
703-838-0355
redbarnmercantile.com

Williams & Sherrill
2003 Huguenot Rd.
Richmond, VA 23235
804-320-1730
williamsandsherrill.com

Willis Furniture Co.
4220 Virginia Beach Blvd.
Virginia Beach, VA 23452
757-340-2112
willisfurniture.com

MIDWEST
Illinois

Bedside Manor
Four locations in Illinois
800-485-4744
shopbedside.com

Bramble
115 N. Oak Park Ave.
Oak Park, IL 60301
708-386-6800
bramble.biz

Chalet Nursery
3132 Lake Ave.
Wilmette, IL 60091
847-256-0561
chaletnursery.com

The Red Balloon Co.
2060 N. Damen Ave.
Chicago, IL 60647
877-969-9800
theredballoon.com

Seagrass
895 Green Bay Rd.
Winnetka, IL 60093
847-446-8444
theseagrasshome.com

Stonehouse
201 Cedar Ave.
St. Charles, IL 60174
630-762-0762
stonehouseoncedar.com

Susan Fredman Design
Group
350 W. Erie St., 1st fl.
Chicago, IL 60654
312-587-8150
susanfredman.com

Twinkle Twinkle Little One
3224 N. Damen Ave.
Chicago, IL 60618
773-472-3000
twinkletwinklelittleone.com

The Uptown Shop
111 E. First St.
Elmhurst, IL 60126
630-832-9200
uptownshop.com

Yvonne Estelle's
11 S. Prospect Ave.
Park Ridge, IL 60068
847-518-1232
yvonne-estelles.com

Indiana

The Red Poppy
2820 Lincoln Ave.
Evansville, IN 47714
812-759-3310

Iowa

American Country
327 Main St.
Ames, IA 50010
800-765-1688
americancountryhome
store.com

Kansas

Annabelles
11547 Ash St.
Leawood, KS 66211
913-345-0606
annabelleslinens.com

Knotty Rug Company
4510 State Line Rd.
Kansas City, KS 66103
913-677-1877
knottyrug.com

Michigan

Bayberry Cottage
510 Phoenix St.
South Haven, MI 49090
269-639-9615
bayberrycottage.com

Bayberry House Interiors
108 N. Park Ave.
Marshall, MI 49068
269-781-7777
bayberryhouseinteriors.com

Cobblestone Rose
101 S. Ann Arbor St.
Saline, MI 48176
734-944-6202
cobblestonerose.com

Cristions
205 N. Old Woodward Ave.
Birmingham, MI 48009
248-723-3337

Cutler's
216 Howard St.
Petoskey, MI 49770
231-347-0341
cutlersonline.com

Gattle's
210 Howard St.
Petoskey, MI 49770
231-347-3982
gattlespetoskey.com

Kramer's Bed, Bath &
Window Fashions
16906 Kercheval Ave.
Grosse Pointe, MI 48230
313-881-9890
kramersbbwf.com

Lemongrass Home
225 Franklin Ave.
Grand Haven, MI 49417
616-842-1992
lemongrasshome.net

Lovell & Whyte
14950 Lakeside Rd.
Lakeside, MI 49116
269-469-5900

Papers Plus
2213 Wealthy St. SE
Grand Rapids, MI 49506
616-458-6116

Third Coast Futons and
Furniture
Shoppes at Romence Village
649 Romence Rd.
Portage, MI 49024
269-323-9667
thirdcoastfutons.com

Minnesota

Alfresco Casual Living
321 S. Main St.
Stillwater, MN 55082
651-439-0814
alfrescocasualliving.com

EuroNest
5700 W. 36th St.
Minneapolis, MN 55416
952-929-2927
euro-nest.com

Market on Union
116 S. Union Ave.
Fergus Falls, MN 56537
218-998-3663

Nola Home
404 Penn Ave. S.
Minneapolis, MN 55405
612-374-4066

Que Sera
3580 Galleria
Edina, MN 55435
952-924-6390

Missouri

Expressions Furniture
7817 Clayton Rd.
St. Louis, MO 63117
314-567-6200

Madison Lane Interiors
505 W. 2nd St.
Joplin, MO 64801
417-206-0550
madisonlaneinteriors.net

Mary Tuttle's
17021 Baxter Rd.
Chesterfield, MO 63005
866-888-8537
marytuttles.com

The Schaefer House
618 Broadway
Jefferson City, MO 65101
573-635-8877
theschaeferhouse.com

Stuff
316 W. 63rd St.
Kansas City, MO 64113
816-361-8222
pursuegoodstuff.com

Nebraska

Pearson & Company
16939 Wright Plaza, no. 143
Omaha, NE 68130
402-932-5999
pearsonandcompany.com

North Dakota

Inspired Interiors
500 20th Ave. SW
Minot, ND 58701
701-838-3636
inspiredinteriorsnd.com

Ohio

Canterbury Home
5648 Main St., no. 2
Sylvania, OH 43560
419-517-4085

Gattle's Inc.
7809A Cooper Rd.
Cincinnati, OH 45242
513-871-4050
gattles.com

KA Menendian Rug Gallery
1090 W. 5th Ave.
Columbus, OH 43212
614-294-3345
karugs.com

Wisconsin

Calico Corners
18525 W. Bluemound Rd.
Brookfield, WI 53045
262-786-4646
calicocorners.com

Cornerstone Shoppe
214 Broad St.
Lake Geneva, WI 53147
262-248-6988
cornerstoneshoppe.com

Door County Nature Works
7798 State Rd. 42
Egg Harbor, WI 54209
920-868-2651
doorcountynatureworks.com

The Home Market
222 E. Erie St.
Milwaukee, WI 53202
414-755-2165
thehomemarket.net

Nest
823 N. 8th St.
Sheboygan, WI 53081
920-803-6378
nesthomestore.com

Past Basket
383 W. Brown Deer Rd.
Milwaukee, WI 53217
414-247-9976
pastbasket.com

Viva La Cabin
10038 Hwy. 57
Sister Bay, WI 54234
920-854-6842

Zander's Interiors
2503 Monroe St.
Madison, WI 53711
608-231-0040
zandersinteriors.com

SOUTHWEST

Arizona

Blueseeds
4108 E. Indian School Rd.
Phoenix, AZ 85018
602-952-1342

Bungalow
15330 N. Hayden Rd.
Scottsdale, AZ 85260
480-948-5409
bungalowaz.com

J Renee Fine Linens
7121 N. Oracle Rd.
Tucson, AZ 85704
520-219-1515
jreneeonline.com

New Mexico

American Country
Collection
620 Cerrillos Rd.
Santa Fe, NM 87505
505-984-0955
accsantafe.com

Leslie Flynt
225 Canyon Rd. S.
Santa Fe, NM 87501
505-955-9901
leslieflynt.com

Oklahoma

Designer Rugs and Import
Group
7118 N. Western Ave.
Oklahoma City, OK 73116
405-842-9000
designerrugsok.com

KS Designs
4209 N. Western Ave.
Oklahoma City, OK 73118
405-524-7868
ksdesignokc.com

Texas

Alyson Jon Interiors
6430 Phelan Blvd.
Beaumont, TX 77706
409-866-3171
alysonjon.com

Back Home Furniture
4477 S. Lamar Blvd.
Austin, TX 78745
512-327-7753
backhomefurniture.com

Bay Window Downtown
705 Hwy. 35 N.
Rockport, TX 78382
361-790-7025

Chiffoniers
3811 Camp Bowie Blvd.
Fort Worth, TX 76107
817-731-8545

The Heirloom Bed Co.
1160 N. Loop 1604 W.
San Antonio, TX 78248
210-694-9200
heirloombeds.com

Hollyhocks
3521 34th St.
Lubbock, TX 79410
806-780-8787
hollyhocksgifts.com

Honey's Home + Style
1706 Austin Ave.
Waco TX, 76710
254-754-3311
honeys-home-style.com

Jabberwocky
105 N. Llano St.
Fredericksburg, TX 78624
830-997-7071

Kem's Bed & Bath
7306 SW 34th, no. 10
Amarillo, TX 79121
806-353-9129

Kuhl-Linscomb
2424 W. Alabama
Houston, TX 77098
713-526-6000
kuhl-linscomb.com

Le Ragge Rugs
1111 W. Hwy. 290 West
Dripping Springs, TX 78620
512-894-0350
cowgirlsandlace.com

Loft
3306 Esperanza Crossing
Austin, TX 78758
512-377-6857
lofthome.com

Make Mine Country
3744 S. Alameda
Corpus Christi, TX 78411
361-225-3744
gatheringsonalameda.com

Mary Cates & Co.
5370 W. Lovers Ln.
Dallas, TX 75209
214-871-7953

My Favorite Room
1029 E. 15th St.
Plano, TX 75074
972-801-4901
kbmdesigns.com

Old Bryan Market Place
202 Bryan Ave.
Bryan, TX 77803
979-779-3245
oldbryanmarketplace.net

Peach Tree Gift Gallery
210 S. Adams St.
Fredericksburg, TX 78624
830-997-9527
peach-tree.com

The Sawmill
4120 Washington Blvd.
Beaumont, TX 77705
409-840-9663
thesawmill.us

Three Doors
2402 Bissonnet St.
Houston, TX 77005
713-528-7800
threedoorshouston.com

Topsy Turvy
334 S. Main St.
Boerne, TX 78006
830-249-0677

Uptown Country Home
3419 Milton St.
Dallas, TX 75205
877-232-2042
uptowncountryhome.com

WEST

California
Daisy's on Park
1347 Park St.
Alameda, CA 94501
510-522-6443

Dream at H.D. Buttercup
3220 Helms Ave.
Los Angeles, CA 90034
310-945-5418
hdbuttercup.com

Misto Lino
3585 Mt. Diablo Blvd.
Lafayette, CA 94549
925-284-6565
mistolino.com

Misto Lino
704 Sycamore Valley Rd. W.
Danville, CA 94526
925-837-6575
mistolino.com

The Quilted Monkey
1112 Montana Ave.
Santa Monica, CA 90403
310-587-1566
thequiltedmonkey.com

Sonoma Home
497 1st St. W.
Sonoma, CA 95476
707-939-6900
sonomahomeonline.com

Summer House
21 Throckmorton Ave.
Mill Valley, CA 94941
415-383-0157

Sunrise Home
831 B St.
San Rafael, CA 94901
415-456-3939
sunrisehome.com

Tumbleweed & Dandelion
1502 Abbot Kinney Blvd.
Venice, CA 90291
310-450-4310
tumbleweedanddandelion
.com

Tuscan Gardens
316 B St.
Petaluma, CA 94952
707-765-2993
tuscangarden.com

Urban Mercantile
2 Henry Adams St.
San Francisco, CA 94103
415-643-6372
urbanmercantile.com

Warmth Company
140 Post Office Dr.
Aptos, CA 95003
831-688-3200
warmthcompany.com

Colorado
The Bunny Gate
719 S. University Blvd.
Denver, CO 80209
303-733-2666

Matelasse
5914 S. Holly St.
Greenwood Villa, CO 80111
720-493-1799

Scandia Down
250 Fillmore St.
Denver, CO 80206
303-355-3510

Idaho
Ketchum Bed and Bath
351 N. Leadville Ave.
Ketchum, ID 83340
208-726-7779

Montana
Amira Rug Gallery
101 S. Higgins
Missoula, MT 59802
406-728-9423
amiraruggallery.com

Oregon
At Home on Oak Street
105 Oak St.
Hood River, OR 97031
541-386-6687

Edman Fine Furniture
110 Oakway Rd.
Eugene, OR 97401
541-683-1886
edmanfurniture.com

Home at Last
1815 NE Broadway
Portland, OR 97212
503-249-4050
dbhomeatlast.com

Le Domaine
7755 Hwy. 101
Gleneden Beach, OR 97388
541-764-3833

Maizey's
90 N. Pioneer St.
Ashland, OR 97520
541-482-6771
maizeys.net

MKID-Montgomery Klash
Interior Design
1111 SW Alder St.
Portland, OR 97205
503-224-7797
montgomeryklash.com

Passion Flower Design
128 E. Broadway
Eugene, OR 97401
541-344-3857
passionflowerdesign.com

Sesame and Lilies
183 N. Hemlock St.
Cannon Beach, OR 97110
503-436-2027
sesameandlilies.com

Utah
Details
1993 S. 1100 E.
Salt Lake City, UT 84105
801-364-8963
detailscomforts.com

Washington
Embellish
285 Winslow Way E.
Bainbridge Island, WA
98110
206-780-2592

CANADA
Cocoon Furnishing
2640 Bristol Circle, no. 20
Oakville, ON L6H 6Z7
905-829-2780
cocoonfurnishings.ca

Elte Linens
80 Ronald Ave.
Toronto, ON M6E 5A2
416-785-7885
elte.com

Muskoka Living Interiors
3655 Hwy. 118 W. RR2
Port Carling, ON P0B 1J0
705-765-6840
muskokaliving.ca

Peaks & Rafters Furniture
Design
162 Medora St.
Port Carling, ON P0B 1J0
705-765-6868
peaksandrafters.com

Union Lighting
1491 Castlefield Ave.
Toronto, ON M6M 1Y3
416-652-2200
unionlightingand
furnishings.com

VIRGIN ISLANDS
Welcome Home
6200 Estate Smith Bay, Ste. 5
St. Thomas, VI 00802
340-776-8652

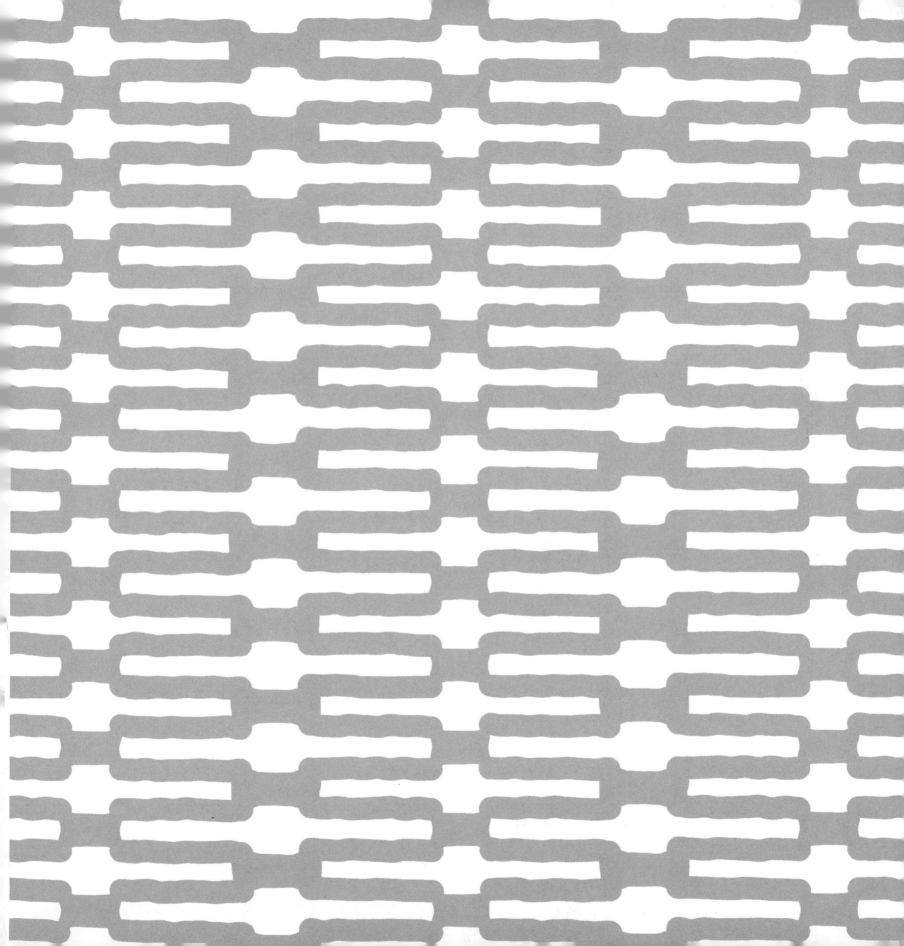

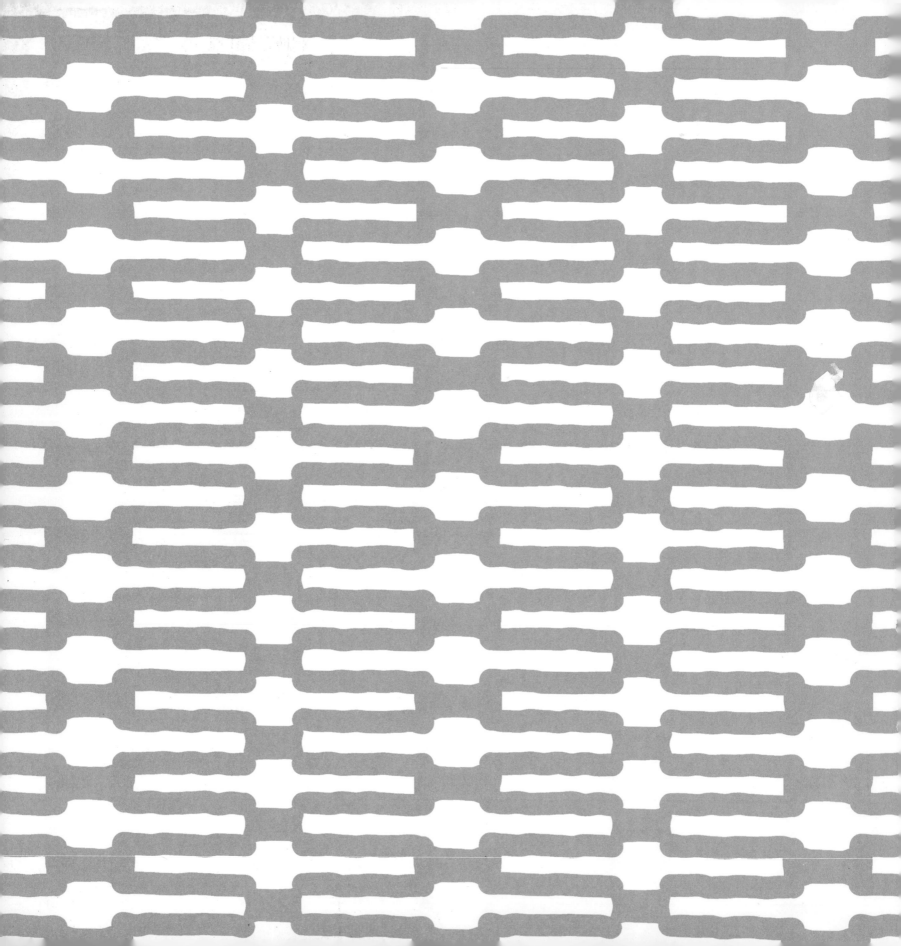